My Father came
from Italy

My Father Came from Italy

BY MARIA COLETTA MCLEAN

RAINCOAST BOOKS

Vancouver

Copyright © 2000 by Maria Coletta McLean

Raincoast Books acknowledges the ongoing support of The Canada Council; the British Columbia Ministry of Small Business, Tourism and Culture through the BC Arts Council; and the Government of Canada through the Book Publishing Industry Development Program (BPIDP).

First published in 2000 by

Raincoast Books
9050 Shaughnessy Street
Vancouver, B.C.
V6P 6E5
(604) 323-7100

www.raincoast.com

Edited by Joy Gugeler
Typeset by Les Smith
Cover photo by Joseph Squillante/photonica
Cover design by Les Smith

1 2 3 4 5 6 7 8 9 10

canadian cataloguing in publication data

McLean, Maria Coletta, 1946-
  My father came from Italy

ISBN 1-55192-356-4

1. McLean, Maria Coletta, 1946- 2. Coletta, Mezzabotte—Journeys—Italy.
3. Fathers and daughters. 4. Italian Canadians—Biography. 5. Supino
(Italy)—Biography. I. Title.
FC106.I8Z7 2000   306.874'2'092   C00-910713-4
F1035.I8M34 2000

Printed and bound in Canada

To my father,
who came from Italy and
shared his stories —
con amore

In the Shadow of Santa Serena

In my father's village, the townspeople tell the story of how Supino got its name. Over 2,000 years ago, Christ walked the dusty road from Rome to Naples and, weary and in need of rest, He paused halfway along the route to look out over a pasture, freckled with clover and buttercups. The late afternoon sun sent the shadow of the Santa Serena across the valley and into the meadow. A wind, fresh and clean, whispered along the ground where He stood. He lay on His back in the soft grass and spread His arms wide to catch the breeze. From the trees came the song of Italian warblers and canaries and the heady scent of burgundy cherries. The aroma of clover perfumed the air and honeybees heavy with sweet pollen buzzed around His head. Christ slept. He woke refreshed, returned to the road and continued on His way.

In the early evening, the sky streaked with purple clouds, the shepherds came to the field to gather their sheep and saw the imprint of His body impressed upon the grasses: two lines intersecting in a giant cross. Day after

day, His imprint remained a testament to the afternoon
He lay, supine, the lines of His body extending to the four
corners of the valley. The farmers from surrounding fields
decided to build four churches: one at the base of the
Santa Serena mountain where He had laid His head;
another in the pasture at His feet; and one at the tips of
the fingers of each of His hands, near clusters of cherry
trees. Christ's imprint lingered on long after the churches
were erected. He held them in the palm of His hands.
Between the churches they built a village with two intersecting streets. They named the village Supino, the Italian
word for supine, for this was the spot Christ had reclined,
His face to the heavens.

I never intended to go to Supino. However, one day Bob,
my husband, came home from a city council meeting and
announced, "The City of York's twinned with a city in Italy
called L'Aquila. The council's going over in November.
What do you think?"

"Well, it sounds interesting," I began. "Who's showing
you around? Do you have an itinerary?"

"I meant what do you think about going with me?"

"I don't know. Will every minute be budgeted, planned?
Will we have to smile and shake hands with strangers all
day?"

"I don't know. Maybe...but it's Italy. You've always
wanted to go. Opportunity is knocking," Bob declared.

The itinerary arrived the following week, written in
Italian and English. Two pages. Morning obligations began

at 9:30 a.m. and the last event of the day got under way at 8:00 p.m. Bob assured me I didn't have to attend everything, then proceeded to point out all the things I wouldn't want to miss.

"You can't count the dinners," he said. "You have to eat anyway."

Dinners were sponsored by different organizations — the Builder's Association or the Abruzzo parliament. Mornings entailed a visit to a medieval Spanish castle or the new Gallucci Supermarket. In between were numerous activities that required endless handshaking and talking to strangers.

"I don't know...," I began.

"I brought you a surprise," Bob said. From behind his back he presented a package with a green, red and white striped cover and the words "Learn to Speak Italian in 20 Easy Lessons" emblazoned across the top, containing two cassettes. "I thought we'd keep one at home and one in the car. We'll be talking like locals in no time," he promised.

The next day, I went to the seniors' drop-in centre to visit my father and told him about the tapes. He nodded and when I asked him what he thought he said, "*Someone should know my language.*" His eyes filled with tears. Guiltily, I began to tell him about the trip to L'Aquila.

"You remember your cousin Guido?" he asked me. "He lives in Rome. He can tell you how to get to Supino."

"I don't think we'll have time to visit your village."

"It's not far," he assured me. "Guido can take you."

"It's not that. It's just that we can't really go off on our

3

own. This trip is an official visit. The itinerary has been set by the Italian government."

"Go on Sunday. Everyone's home with their family on Sunday."

I laughed, but I checked the itinerary and of course Sunday was free. "Does Guido speak English?"

"Sure."

Later that evening, Bob and I got out the map of Italy and tried to find Supino; even though there were dozens of towns south of Rome, Supino was not among them. Bob resorted to a more detailed map of the Lazio region; no Supino. Finally, we peered through a magnifying glass; Supino was not there.

"How big *is* Supino?"

"Pretty big," he said. "Maybe 100 families. You don't need the map. Your cousin can show you. You remember Guido, don't you?"

"He's the cousin who lived in Toronto for a few years?"

"Right. You call him. He'll meet you and take you right to the village."

"I haven't seen Guido for 30 years. How old was I when he went back to the old country? Eight? How's he going to recognize me?"

"Wear your Canada pin. He'll find you okay."

"And where is Supino, exactly?"

"Take the road from Rome to Naples," my father said. "About halfway there, turn right. That's Supino."

On the first Sunday in Italy, Rocco, our Toronto travel

agent who also owned a summer home in Supino and was in Italy at the same time we were, made a long-distance call from L'Aquila to Rome, arranging to meet Guido at the main bus terminal there in front of the water fountain, at noon. We took the bus from the main *piazza* in L'Aquila, winding through several mountain tunnels, vineyards and olive groves. At an intersection just outside Rome, a donkey pulling a cart of wicker baskets brimming with olives reminded me that there was an olive grove on my father's family farm. Perhaps they would be pressing the olives while we were there.

I hadn't seen Guido since I was a young girl, but I remembered he looked exactly like my father: a short, white-haired Italian with callused hands and a creased face from too many hours under the garden sun. As I searched among the hundreds of faces in the terminal that day I realized that every Italian man of a certain age fit that description. I walked around the water fountain a few times, my Canada flag clutched in my hand, hoping my cousin would step out of the crowd and introduce himself. An hour and a half passed and still no Guido. We sat on the edge of the fountain like orphans deposited on a doorstep.

Finally, from out of the crowd, a man walked quickly toward us. A package of Player's cigarettes and a clip-on pen stuck out of his shirt pocket.

Guido shook my hand, kissed my cheeks. "Maria," he said. "Welcome."

"Welcome" seemed to be the only English word Guido remembered. After that, he spouted a stream of Italian;

I didn't understand any of it. And Bob was no help at all.

"Ask him where his car is," Bob said.

I didn't have a wide vocabulary, but managed to determine that Guido was walking, not driving, so I had no idea how he was going to take us to Supino. Guido took my arm and lead us to the taxi stand. In a few minutes we were whipping through Rome's traffic.

"We're taking a cab to Supino?" asked Bob.

"Apparently."

Apparently not, because within five minutes, we pulled up in front of an apartment building in downtown Roma and Guido motioned us to get out.

"Does Guido understand that he's supposed to take us to Supino?" Bob asked.

"I don't know, Bob. He is two hours late. Obviously he doesn't own a car. I don't know what we're doing here. Want to hear something funny? Do you know what the name Guido means in Italian?"

"Man who doesn't speak English?" suggested Bob.

"Guide."

Although Guido wasn't a great linguist, he was brimming with good will. He put an arm around each of our shoulders as he led us through a gate to a courtyard garden, red roses still blooming defiantly in the late November sunlight. In the centre was a willowy tangerine tree, its boughs extended languid and leafless, but heavy with fruit, vibrant orange skins radiant in the pale daylight.

Guido held open a brass, folding elevator door and we stepped inside. After a few bells and several lurches, we arrived on the fourth floor to the intoxicating aroma of tomatoes and herbs. A few steps down the hall an apartment door was open and voices rose up to greet us. Inside, the dining room table was extended from the front hall into the living room, encircled by chairs and benches and stools. Strangers shook our hands, kissed us, spoke to us in Italian. A woman came from the kitchen, kissed Bob, pointed to her wedding band, saying, "Guido" and then to herself, "Luigina," waved a bag of spaghetti and put a tumbler of vermouth in my hand. Seconds later the phone rang and Guido was motioning to me, "Maria, *telefono.*"

"*Per me?*"

"You don't know me," began the woman on the phone, who explained that a lunch had been prepared for us, after which Guido would take us to Supino in a small rented van. It came with a driver because Guido didn't drive. The driver was supposed to pick us up at the apartment at two o'clock.

"It's twenty to three," Bob pointed out when I relayed the information.

"I know."

It was four o'clock and the sky was grey by the time lunch was finished. If we didn't get to Supino soon, it would be dark and we wouldn't be able to see anything. The doorbell rang several times, but it was only another lunch guest arriving. Guido was smoking by the courtyard gate when the van arrived a half an hour later. We kissed Luigina on the way out, "*Grazie, grazie,*" and flew down the stairs to the sidewalk.

"How far to Supino?" I asked, pointing to my watch.

"*Un'ora,*" said Guido, holding up one finger, and within

minutes we were on the *autostrada* speeding south. In 50 minutes, we turned right at the Frosinone exit. The driver slowed down at the tollbooth where he passed some lire notes to the tollbooth operator, shook his head in disgust, muttered *"ladro"* under his breath and drove off.

Bob looked at me. "Thief," I explained.

"Bloody thief," clarified Guido.

As the sun slid toward Santa Serena we sped past a dozen farms, olive and fruit trees dotting the landscape and low stone houses at the end of driveways lined with grapevines. Suddenly the driver stopped, beside a driveway near a flock of sheep grazing freely beneath sprawling cherry trees. A long path of dusty grapevines, heavy with burgundy fruit, led to a stone farmhouse. Smoke spiralled from the chimney. Warm yellow light glowed from the windows. The front door was framed by an arbour of red roses. I remember being told my grandmother had planted them close to the front door; she kept the door open so she could enjoy their fragrance.

"Is this it?" I asked.

"*Sí, sí,*" assured Guido, but he wasn't talking about the farm, he was pointing to a sign that read: QUATTRO STRADE. Four streets. When my father had talked about this intersection, he had said, "I used to take the cow down to the four streets," or "I had a friend who lived outside of town, near the four streets," and I had always thought he'd forgotten their names. He hadn't said this *was* the name. The fourth street went straight uphill into Supino Centro so we continued along it for 10 minutes through an archway of trees, the late afternoon sunlight filtering through the branches, their leaves brushing the top of the car as we rounded the curve. We paused while the driver honked to his friends sitting outside a bar and Guido said to us, *"Benvenuto a Supino."*

The main street was a marriage of ancient houses and stores. Red geraniums and black-clad grandmothers leaned out of every window. This narrow street, Via Regina Margherita, had been named for the queen of Italy, but was made for pedestrians, donkey carts and wheelbarrows. Compact cars could manoeuvre the narrow passageway one lane at a time; small vans could get by if they folded in their side mirrors. Trucks and buses had to park at the base of the hill in front of the Church of San Sebastiano. We drove up the steep cobblestone street, one eye on the orange ball of the sun, the other on the red orb of the traffic light. Out the passenger-side window, so close you could reach out and touch it, there was a hardware store. A man in a white apron stood on the top step smoking. He and Guido carried on a conversation while villagers walked past on their way to the shops and we waited impatiently for the light to change.

I called out to the driver, *"Attenzione.* Red light, *rossa."* But he merely shrugged his shoulders and switched gears. Guido turned up the palm of his hand, pointed toward the front windshield. "Nobody comes," he explained. Traffic lights in Italy are negotiable.

The buildings were tall, slim, three or four stories high and so close to the road I felt that I was passing through a long, unlit tunnel. At the end of the street, the late afternoon sun shone on a *piazza.* The road here would have become four lanes if someone hadn't built a shoe store in the centre of the square. On the left, the Santa Serena mountain and the Church of San Nicola were separated by a worn and narrow path where goats, their copper bells glinting in the twilight, walked single file. We, however, took the road to the right, zigzagging ever upward until we arrived at a driveway and ground to a stop. Many unknown relations spilled from the doorways of a modern cement home, where my cousin Dina and her family lived on the first floor and her brother Antonio's family lived on the second. They began talking quickly and simultaneously, interrupted only by emphatic hand gestures. Seven Italians speaking, no one listening. Surrounded by new-found family, we were corralled toward the wire fence adjoining my father's property. *"Eccola.* There it is! Your father's farm."

"This?" I asked, pointing to a small stone structure, about the size of a garden shed, and a tiny fenced yard.

"Sí, sí," he nodded.

Everything my father described was here, but in miniature. The farmhouse was no bigger than a one-car garage; the roof no taller than my father himself — five foot two. There was no cherry orchard, in fact, only one cherry tree hugged the side of the house, its branches hanging low over the red clay roof. Behind the house were three olive trees. Father had said he and his brothers were allowed to sleep outside in the nice weather, from the time the blue wildflowers bloomed on the mountainside until their father had pressed the olives and crushed the grapes. I had imagined them carrying handmade quilts and a woven wicker picnic basket out to an olive grove.

I glanced at Guido, who stood with his hands in his pockets, nodding his head. I looked at Bob. He merely lifted his camera and focused on the stonework of the little house. I stared at the low building made of rocks and stones and patches of cement and wondered how my grandparents had raised five children there. Four plump brown chickens high-stepped between the olive trees, scratching for bugs in the cool November evening. A square of light from the house next door highlighted a single antique rose vine a few inches from the front door. Smoke spiralled from nearby chimneys, smelling of beech-nut and oak. My father's house looked cold and dark and empty. Still, I longed to go inside. I listened for voices of the past, whispers from a house once alive with the sounds of ancestors. But it remained silent, perhaps waiting for my father rather than this tall Canadian woman who claimed to be a part of the Coletta family. The sun slid beneath the curve of the mountain and in the cool, damp air I felt only loneliness.

"Come," said Guido. "Your cousin Dina made coffee."

I bent close to the farmhouse wall, wiggled a small stone from beside a loose chunk of cement and put it in my pocket. The stone was surprisingly warm.

Next door at Dina's, four children examined us from the bench beside the fireplace: Dina's two sons and Antonio's two daughters. Curious because we were family, but awed because we had come from Canada. And as I smiled at the silent children I remembered something from Guido's visit to Toronto and the Sundays we shared during his two-year stay in Canada. He could be counted upon to put his hand inside his jacket pocket and remove a rectangular package wrapped in shiny paper with letters embossed in gold. Jersey Milk. We had waited, looking at him like these young cousins sitting on the bench were watching us now. "*Mangia. Mangia,*" he would say, "Eat!" The warm milky chocolate, soft from its long ride on the bus in Guido's jacket pocket. What would these children remember? I rummaged in my purse, found rolls of cherry Lifesavers and gave them to the children. Holding the unfamiliar candy in their hands, they stared at me.

"*Mangia. Mangia,*" said Guido.

The children slipped off the wrappers, unrolled the shiny silver paper, crunched their candy and continued to stare. I checked my Italian phrase book, then asked the children their ages. "*Quant'anni hai?*" They looked at each other, then at Guido. Guido repeated the phrase, running the words together. The children nodded their heads, called out their ages: *cinque, nove, sette, dodici.* I nodded my head and smiled. Bob knew numbers in Italian, almost as well as he knew them in English. He translated quickly, as if he were bargaining at the local market. "Five, nine, seven and twelve."

I asked the children about school. "*Scuola?*" This time they looked at their respective mothers. There was a quick exchange, consent given and the children bolted from the room. Two minutes later they were back, standing shyly with their school exercise books in their hands. The seven-year-old boy showed me his printing book, pointing proudly to the stamp the teacher had attached: BRAVO!

I saw some crayon drawings, with bright yellow suns in the corners, then studied a few spelling test results. The children crowded around Bob, showing him their math books. Bob took his clue from the teacher's red stamp and repeated, "*Bravo! Bravo!*" Then the room grew silent again.

The house was warm with the aroma of coffee brewing and beechnut logs burning in the fireplace. From the firewood came a low whispering and sometimes a spark to break the silence. I fidgeted, struggling to think of words to string together to pass for conversation. The men smoked cigarettes, the women set out espresso cups, arranged cookies on a tray. I tried to speak to them, but my Italian was halting and uncertain. I relied on my Italian-English dictionary and various hand gestures.

"It's okay," reassured Guido. "*Mangia il tuo biscotto.* Eat your biscuit."

Outside the kitchen window, the starless sky stood in contrast to a faint curved line that was the peak of Santa Serena. A tightness grew in my throat as I looked around the kitchen. Had my father sat like this with his parents and his brothers and sisters, watching the fire on a cool November evening? Guido put his hands on his knees, got up slowly. He looked at me, his head tipped slightly to one side. He raised his shoulders, turned up the palms of his hands. His eyes were the same clear, watery blue as my father's. It was time to go. I held my dictionary in my hand, felt the slippery plastic cover and knew the words I wanted to express could not be found inside its pages. I wished my father were with us. He could have spoken to them; the silences wouldn't have bothered *him*. I removed the

Canada pin from my lapel and attached it to Antonio's sweater. Slipping off my earrings, tiny amber droplets of stained glass wrapped in gold, I put them in the hand of Dina. Bob pinned Canada pins on everyone as they kissed him on both cheeks and pumped his hand. He gave paper flags to the children. They held them solemnly, the youngest child waving his flag smoothly, like a silent metronome. Moving quickly from one to another, I shook hands, kissed cheeks. There were tears in my cousins' eyes, but I didn't allow myself to see them.

I waved to the two rows of adults and children standing in the driveway — every relative with an arm around another — until the van began its downward spiral through the narrow streets of Supino.

The next day we toured the Basilica of Collemaggio in L'Aquila. Our guide pointed out architectural details, gave the history of paintings and statues. We went to the San Filippo Theatre as well, sitting in the front row as guests of honour at a children's play. Students from a nearby school tromped in, their cheeks rosy, stuffed knapsacks beneath their seats as they settled down to watch the puppets on stage. When the Nutcracker fought with the mice, the children cheered his every move, calling, *"Bravo! Bravo!"* During the lunch at the Cogefar company cafeteria and the Duca Abruzzi Hotel press conference and the Centi Palace meeting with the premier of the Abruzzo region, I thought of Supino and my father. I saw images of my father everywhere: a man walking across a field with his hand in his pocket had his same steady pace. A man in a blue work shirt fixing a fence reached into his pocket and pulled out a small penknife. It had a yellowed mother-of-pearl handle like my father's.

These memories accompanied me to Toronto. When friends asked about our trip to Italy, I spoke only about Supino, a village of perhaps 1,000 people, without a cinema, restaurant, theatre. Not even a *bocce* court. I knew from Rocco's descriptions that every day the old men gather at the *piazza* beside the Church of Santa Maria Maggiore to read the newspaper, drink small cups of strong black coffee, argue politics and soccer. As the months passed, and the sun grew weaker, the length of the buildings' shadows grew longer and the old men moved down the steep hill to the square in front of San Sebastiano to continue their conversations. The villagers still walked up the cobblestone street each day to collect cold spring water from the fountain at the base of the mountain. The stream passed underground, heading down Via Condotto Vecchio to the corner at Via D'Italia where neighbours stood on summer evenings in the path of the cooling breeze. *Fresca.* On the outskirts of town, families built sprawling pastel-coloured villas with arches and elaborate wrought-iron fences. In the corners stood the original structures of their parents' homes. It is Supino law that you can build on, but you cannot tear down, existing buildings, so every new Supinese home is technically an addition to an existing one. The new home represented the villagers' prosperity while also acknowledging their origins. "Success built with humility." Rocco had told me all of this while we waited at Leonardo da Vinci Airport for our return flight.

Supino was almost medieval, a village stopped in time. Unreal. I framed the photo of my father's home and put it on the mantle next to the piece of rock I had taken from its foundation. In quiet moments, just before I fell asleep, I thought I could hear Supino calling me. The cool wind that came down from the Santa Serena, used my Italian name: *Maria*.

I thought of myself as Canadian. I'd always said, "My father came from Italy, but I was born here." Since I'd been to Supino, I felt differently. My father came by himself in February 1927. He was almost 19. The day he had left Supino was the last time he saw his parents. His father had said to him, "Don't forget. Send money." His mother said nothing. She just cried.

When the *Marloch* docked in Sydney, Nova Scotia and my father disembarked it was the first time he had seen snow. And it was cold. He had on only a woollen jacket, with a passport and three dollars in his pocket. He didn't speak any English. My father took the train from Halifax to Union Station in Toronto where Regina met him. My father lived with my aunt Regina and uncle Lawrence in their house on Dundas Avenue. It had a fruit and vegetable store in the living room and a bicycle in the shed out the back. Every morning, Lawrence would pedal down to the Food Terminal on the Lakeshore and return with a day's supply of produce that Regina sold while watching their daughter Rose. My father got a job with a construction company, driving a truck. This pattern continued for two years until Regina had a second daughter, Cecilia. They gave up the store and the whole family moved to a larger house on Geoffrey Street. My father lived there for the next 12 years in the third-floor attic. He cooked in the summer and froze in the winter and bumped his head on the angled ceiling all year long. His years there were happy ones, visiting with friends on the weekends, playing cards, going to the movies, entertaining his nieces.

Eventually my father switched from driving a truck for the construction company to driving a truck for Toronto Macaroni. Here, he met my mother; she was working in the office. They went out on a bet. My mother's girlfriends dared her to go out with him, an immigrant and a truck driver. My mother had wanted to make her current boyfriend jealous because it was wartime and he wanted to wait until after the war to marry. My mother was 25, my father was 34. He offered her an engagement ring and she took it. A marriage built on spite.

My father continued to drive a truck for Toronto Macaroni, delivering boxes of pasta to Italian supermarkets all over Ontario. Before my mother turned 30, she had my brother Don, my sister Linda and me. He was gone before we got up for school and often not home for dinner. I remember the sound of his black metal lunch box as he sat it on the kitchen counter, the slight scrape of the chair as he pulled it up to the mother-of-pearl Arborite table, the way he slipped some vegetables off my sister's plate onto his own because she hated to eat them. Sometimes he'd tell us about his trip to Sudbury, Thunder Bay, Sault

Ste. Marie. The boss always gave him money for meals and a motel on these long trips, but he took his lunches, skipped the comfort of a motel whenever he could and drove straight through. That's how he managed, sometimes, to make it home for dinner the next day.

One Saturday afternoon when my older brother, Don, was at the movies with his friends and my mother had gone shopping, my father took my sister Linda and me to the factory. We drove into its gravel parking lot and before my father was out of the car, a man with a bushy moustache called out to him. "Loreto," the man shouted, a greeting and an announcement. My father held our hands and introduced us to the moustached man who bowed while we scuffed our shoes on the pavement. In his boss' office — a crowded little room with a desk piled with invoices, a glass ashtray and a crucifix — another man shook hands with us and gave us a candy from his desk drawer. The telephone kept ringing and he kept answering it, saying, "*Aspetta.*" He'd talk for a minute, everything in Italian, hang up and the phone would ring again.

We went up a narrow set of stairs and, since we were wearing our Sunday dresses from Regina, we held our crinoline skirts close to our legs so we wouldn't get them dirty. We entered a large warm room, full of the moist smell of eggs, flour dust dancing in the sunlight streaming through the windows. Spaghetti, linguine, and their fatter cousin fettuccine hung over wooden dowelling in row after row, up and down the length of the room. My father explained that this was the drying room and when the spaghetti was ready, they'd whack it with a flat stick to break it into lengths, then slide it into packages. Downstairs at the loading dock my father shook hands with all his co-workers and then lifted us into the cab of his truck to let us pretend we were driving.

The years passed. My father continued to drive for the Toronto Macaroni factory and the year Don started Weston Collegiate, we moved to the town of Weston. Don and Linda and I spent our teenage years there and our parents' lives faded into the background as we graduated and married and began families of our own. The year my father turned 65, the Toronto Macaroni factory retired him, presenting him with an engraved silver tray: Loreto Coletta. But my father continued driving, delivering flowers for his nephew Joe until he had a stroke. A few years later, my parents bought the little bungalow next door to our house on King Street and that October our youngest daughter, Kathryn, was born.

By the spring, my father had recovered enough to help Bob build an addition to our house and to make a path of cement stones from our front door to theirs. It was my father, perhaps with some urging from our older children, who bought four giant cement foot prints at the garden centre and lay two at the bottom of his verandah pointing toward our house and placed the other two at the end of our path pointing back to theirs. All of the grandchildren would, in turn, position their small sneakered feet on the giant footprints and as my father called, "Go," hop back and forth between homes on one foot. When they grew tired of this, my father assisted them in the building of a human pyramid, positioning the oldest four cousins in a row on their hands and knees, three smaller cousins on their backs, then two more on a third tier and finally baby Kathryn on top.

That summer my father, Don and Bob turned under most of the back lawn of my father's house to make a vegetable garden. Every time my father went to visit one of his nephews, he'd return with vegetable seeds tucked inside an old envelope or a basket full of drooping plants. The next day we'd find space between the rows for cantaloupe seeds or garlic plants or a few acorn squash. We spent long mornings planting tomato and pepper seedlings, weeding the lettuce, onion and spinach rows. Kathryn passed those mornings in her playpen under the shade of the peach tree as my father told us the stories of his boyhood. These he repeated time and again so as to re-live the memories. All I had to do was listen and laugh in the right spots.

We spent half a dozen summers in this way. My father hung a rope in the sturdy branches of the flowering crab-apple tree, notched two triangular pieces from a scrap of two-by-four and made a swing for Kathryn. As he pushed her he led her in a song he'd create on the spot. Every day the words changed, but the last line was always, "because I love you."

By the time Kathryn started school, my father was showing the usual signs of age, preferring to sit on a lawn chair while Linda and I gardened. Each year we added a strip of sod to the vegetable garden making it a little smaller and I started planting a row of flowers here and there among the vegetables. My father never liked the flowers. "You can't eat flowers," he'd remind me and I'd say, "These marigolds keep the aphids away from the tomato plants." He'd just shake his head.

The last year we had the garden Kathryn's kindergarten class was studying vegetables. Her class visited our garden because some of the children had never seen vegetables, except in the grocery store, and wanted to pick a ripe tomato or pull a carrot. Linda and I weeded the garden carefully and I planted a few yellow chrysanthemums to fill in some of the spaces left by harvested lettuce and peas. My father shook his head again, but planted some surprises of his own in any case: a row of lollipops to trick the children.

I was remembering this as I sat with my father at the seniors' drop-in centre one dreary February day a few years after his stroke and a few months after we had returned from Italy.

He said, "If I was home, the flowers would just be coming out on the mountain." Whenever my father spoke of home I knew he didn't mean Toronto, he meant Supino.

"Already?" I asked. "It's only February."

"Sure. Soon as the sun shines on that side of the mountain, the blue flowers pop up everywhere. I used to bring them to my mother."

"Was it the first sign of spring?"

"As soon as the flowers bloomed, we were allowed to sleep outside." My father stretched his arms, as if remembering the freedom of sleeping in the backyard instead of cramped in the farmhouse. But I had seen the backyard of that farmhouse.

"Where did you sleep?"

"You saw the farm," said my father. "Three brothers, three trees."

I remembered those ancient olive trees and tried to picture three brothers fashioning beds in their branches. I thought back to the night we left my cousin's house in Supino. When the driver had stopped beside the Bar Italia, the headlights of the van illuminated an open doorway across the street. A cobbler sat at his workbench, mending a work boot under a single lightbulb. His hair was perfectly white, like my father's.

"There's an old shoemaker in Supino, near the Bar Italia."

"That's Antonio, or maybe his brother Primo."

"I thought he might have made the shoes for you and your brothers and sisters when you lived in Supino."

"*Nonno* made our shoes."

"Your grandfather? I thought he was blind."

"Well sure, but he could carve. He carved the soles from wood and put leather straps on them."

"Like sandals?" I asked. "What about the winter?"

"We wore wool socks. My mother knit them. If it was really cold, we wore two pair. We liked to play a trick on him in the fall, when the grape leaves withered and fell from the vine. We'd find a brown leaf curled good and tight and your aunt Regina would give it to *nonno* saying it was a cigar. Then we'd run away as fast as we could. *Nonno* was blind, but if he could reach us he'd still cuff us on the head. After he died we missed playing the trick on him — all we could do was crunch the grape leaves under our shoes. It wasn't the same."

I began to see that there was more to these stories and to Supino and to my father than I had ever known. I began to imagine a scheme in which I brought my father to Supino, bought the farmhouse where he was born; we could stay there when we visited. The trip would be for my father, but I would also own a piece of the old country, my country. I knew this was completely unreasonable, but I hadn't made the decision with my mind; I had made it with my heart.

"This idea's going to sound crazy at first," I said to Bob, "but why don't we buy my father's house in Supino? Just a minute. Let me finish. The house is empty. We could leave it the way it is on the outside and have the inside divided into a couple of rooms. We could take him back there for a visit. It would be like a cottage — a cottage in Italy."

Bob didn't say any of the things I expected him to say. He said, "I'll call Rocco and see what he can do."

Bob asked Rocco to approach the people who owned my father's farm and ask if they would sell. A few weeks passed and then Rocco reported that the owners wouldn't sell no matter how much we offered them. I said to tell them we wanted the farm because it belonged to my grandparents, because my father was born in that house, because he left 64 years ago and was still tied to that soil, because I was Supinese. But the owners still said no. I said we only needed to buy the house, they could still use the land with the grapevines and the olive trees. No.

At the same time the Supino wind continued to call to

me, more gently now. One afternoon, in early spring, there was a note on the kitchen counter with just a few words written hurriedly on the back of a used envelope: "How does a three-room, three-story house, near the water fountain, just up from the *piazza* sound?" Perhaps it blew in on the wind from the mountaintop.

"How did you find out about this?" I asked Bob.

"The barber told us."

"How does Peter the barber know about a house that's for sale in Supino?"

"Peter the barber was closed today," Bob explained. "So, I took your father to a place up in Woodbridge. I thought he'd enjoy speaking Italian to Lorenzo, the owner. I left him there for an hour while I made some calls. When I came back to pick him up, Lorenzo had given your father all the details about a house in Supino. Its owner is Supinese but he lives here."

Lorenzo came from Supino as well. After the Second World War many of Supino's villagers emigrated to Canada. Brothers and sisters from one family married siblings from another so that if they traced their origins, eventually they'd find that everyone in the village was related. My father knew Lorenzo's family, who had lived close to the Church of Santa Maria Maggiore. Lorenzo knew of a house for sale between there and the Church of San Nicola. I could picture the house: a grapevine growing in the backyard and fragrant red roses climbing up a balcony.

"I think we should buy it," I told Bob.

"I can't buy a house without seeing it!" Bob's not Italian.

"What's the worst that can happen?" I reasoned. "If we don't like it, we'll just sell it again. You can take my father to see the owner. He'll speak to him in Italian and find out everything you want to know." Lorenzo knew the house's owner, Tucci, belonged to the Supino Social Club, begun informally in the 50s as an alternative to hanging around the bars or being told by the police to move along while you were standing on a Toronto sidewalk, talking after a movie, the restaurants and cafés closed. They hadn't gotten around to constructing a building yet, but there was renewed interest in having a permanent location as the 40th anniversary was approaching and there were now over 500 families from Supino in the greater Toronto area. In the meantime, they met here and there. This Friday it would be at the Monte Cassino banquet hall.

That night the parking lot was full and inside everyone was speaking Italian, shouting, tunes on the *organetto* drowned out by protests about which national anthem to play first: music filled the hall with the notes of *"Fratelli d'Italia,"* followed by "O Canada." Then, everyone sat down, uncorked the wine bottles, offered cigarettes to their neighbours and began various conversations. The president of the club began to talk about activities the club had planned for the following year. Every announcement invited a recap of the highlights of last year's picnic, the feast of San Lorenzo, the outdoor mass. As the president continued his speech, the noise and the memories grew louder. Two men near the front of the hall began to tape large sheets of bristol board to the wall. Bob and my father stepped into the lobby to talk with my cousin Johnny. Johnny knew Tucci. "He's my daughter's godfather. He's not here tonight." Johnny knew Tucci's house, but not his address. He could take them there, but it was getting a bit late. Bob and Johnny went inside with my father to say goodbye to Carmen, a friend of Bob's who stopped by my husband's coffee plant on his bus route each week. The atmosphere inside was relaxed. Platters of pizza had joined the wine bottles on the tables. The bartender was beginning to grind the espresso beans. The large sheets of bristol board were covered with names and on each board one name was circled. Under the heading "President" the name "Boni" was circled. Under "Vice-president," "Caprara" was circled. Under "Treasurer" were several names, but the circled name was "McLean."

"*Auguri*," said Carmen, as he shook Bob's hand.

"*Auguri*," said a stranger.

"*Auguri*," said my cousin Augusto.

Bob looked at my father. "Congratulations, you're the new treasurer of the club," he explained, as he pointed toward the voting results marked on the sheets of bristol board.

"I don't speak Ital—" began Bob.

"It's numbers, Bob," assured Carmen. "We write them down for you."

Later Bob relayed the story and explained his plan. "*No problema.* Lorenzo said Tucci goes to the bar at St. Clair and Dufferin every Sunday after church." Bob was so pleased with this key information about the house owner, I didn't have the heart to tell him there are a dozen bars at St. Clair and Dufferin.

The following Sunday, Bob and my father drove to that corner, went in and out of the bars asking for a man named Tucci. They ended up sitting in Tucci's backyard in the warm February sunlight, drinking wine and admiring Tucci's tomato and pepper seedlings growing beneath a greenhouse of two-by-fours and heavy plastic sheeting. My father and Tucci talked about the old country, various relatives and friends from years ago. Tucci gave them some green onions and they had coffee and cookies at the kitchen table.

When they returned I had cream, sugar and cookies on *our* kitchen table. I phoned next door to my mother.

She had come from Italy when she was young as well, but all her memories of the old country were remembrances of hardship: the death of her mother, the years of poverty, the cruelness of a maiden aunt who cared for them and the constant hunger. She didn't want to go back, she wanted to forget. When my father had come to Canada, he was 19 and although his life in Italy had been a poor one, his memories were rich. He always talked about his childhood and his village with tenderness, while my mother spoke only with bitterness.

I was pouring the cream into her coffee, when Bob

asked, "What did the owner say about the condition of the house?"

"I forgot to ask," said my father, laughing and slapping his knee with the palm of his hand.

My mother pushed the plate of cookies toward Bob. "How are your parents?"

"Fine," Bob replied, then turning to my father again he asked. "Didn't he tell you anything at all?"

"He's anxious to sell. His daughter's getting married this year, so he needs the money. Said he'd even take a little less, but he's got to know right away. Raffaele — that's his first name — went back to Supino 15 years ago. Said everything's pretty much the same. They put new plaster on the front of the church — that's all. He said it looked good."

"Would *you* like to go back, for a visit?" I asked, as I passed him the plate of cookies.

"We really don't need to buy a house to take your father back to Supino," interrupted Bob. "There's that *pensione* just outside of the village — or we can stay at a hotel in Frosinone. It's only 30 minutes away."

"Why would you pay money to stay in a hotel if you own a house?" asked my father.

"Would you like to go to Supino?" I asked again.

My father looked at my mother. She had finished her coffee, slid her cup toward the centre of the table. Her arms were crossed against her chest, her lips set.

"Well, it might be good," he began, hesitantly, "to see the old places again. I have some cousins living up on the mountain...."

"They'd all be dead now," interrupted my mother, frowning. She pushed back her chair.

"Maybe. They were younger than me though. They could still be there."

"You don't want to go back," declared my mother. "There's nothing there."

I looked at my father. I looked at Bob to see if he heard it too. In the silence, we knew he wanted to go. Over the years I'd grown used to my mother answering for her husband. She made the decision, but she said, "Your father doesn't want to..." as if he had a choice. Normally, I would have let the idea drop. Experience had taught me that she would get her way in the end. She insisted he didn't want to go, warned me I'd be sorry, money would be wasted, he wouldn't like it, he'd want to come back after one day.

"I'm warning you. If you take him, don't bring him back here." My mother always attached the same string: accept her decision or risk losing her love. "Tell her you don't want to go," she said to my father.

But my father didn't say a word. He just looked at me with pale blue eyes, waiting.

I would have given up if it hadn't been for a cold March night a few weeks later. My father got lost returning from my sister's, just as he had a few months earlier when he walked to Weston and Keele, thinking he still worked at Toronto Macaroni. My father's doctor said it wasn't Alzheimer's, it wasn't dementia, it was the stress of living with my mother. While Bob and I drove around looking for my father we worried that these incidents were happening more frequently, becoming more dangerous. Suddenly Bob slammed on the brakes. Someone was standing in the middle of the road, caught in our headlights. It was my father. A car behind us blew its horn. My father was startled; he looked hurriedly from side to side, but he didn't move. Reaching for the door handle, I opened it noiselessly and walked slowly to the centre lane, motioning to the impatient driver to go ahead. Then, I touched the shoulder of my father's coat, surprised at how feeble he'd become. I kept my voice very soft, tried to sound reassuring.

"Where are you going?" I asked, with a small forced smile. My father looked at me. He didn't know me.

"Where are you going, Dad?" I tried again.

His cheeks and nose were red from the cold. The bitter March wind blew his coat open and I reached out my hand to button it. He flinched. I took a step back, wrapped my arms around my body.

"It's okay," I lied. I could feel the tears, hot and bitter, at the back of my throat. "Can I help you? Where do you want to go?" His gentle blue eyes were rimmed with red and he started to cry.

"I can't find my house," he said, as if I was an interested stranger. "It's number 183, but there's no one home."

"This is Church Street," I explained. "You live on the next street, on King Street."

"My daughter lives next door," he continued. "I knocked at her door, but a woman said no one named Maria lived there. She said she couldn't help me."

Couldn't help me. The words echoed in my head, in my chest. I bit the inside of my lip to keep from sobbing. Someone blew a horn, startling my father again. Taking his arm, I led him to the sidewalk. I could feel his elbow through the coat sleeve. He was trembling. We had crossed to the lawn of the local hospital, the same hospital in which doctors had told me my father suffered the brunt of verbal abuse. I offered my father a ride home; he didn't say no. It was dark, but a little light shone on the verandah of #183. My mother's shadow blocked the doorway.

"You're home," I said to my father.

"Home?" he echoed.

Johnny knew the Tucci family from when he lived in Supino and knew the house on Via Condotto Vecchio. Johnny assured us that not only did the house exist, but he'd been inside. "I was there a few years ago, 14, 15 years. It looked pretty good."

"Does it need work?" Bob asked.

Johnny paused for a moment, considering the question. Then he suggested, "Maybe it's going to need a coat of paint." So with the help of Rocco and a lawyer, *signor* Marcello Renzi, we signed the papers and bought the house at #10 Via Condotto Vecchio. *Signor* Renzi told us the street name meant "the old water way," the path the underground stream followed from the mountain down to the pastures of Supino. In the lawyer's office, our street name sounded romantic and idyllic, but as soon as we shook hands with the owner and handed over the cheque,

I began to have doubts.

Bob said, "It'll be fine. We'll go over in May and take a look at the place. Then we'll hire a painter. You're worrying about nothing. I want to buy this house, for you and for your father. We can give him a trip back to the old country, a few days of happiness in his hometown and memories for the rest of his life. And we will always have it as a reminder of where you came from."

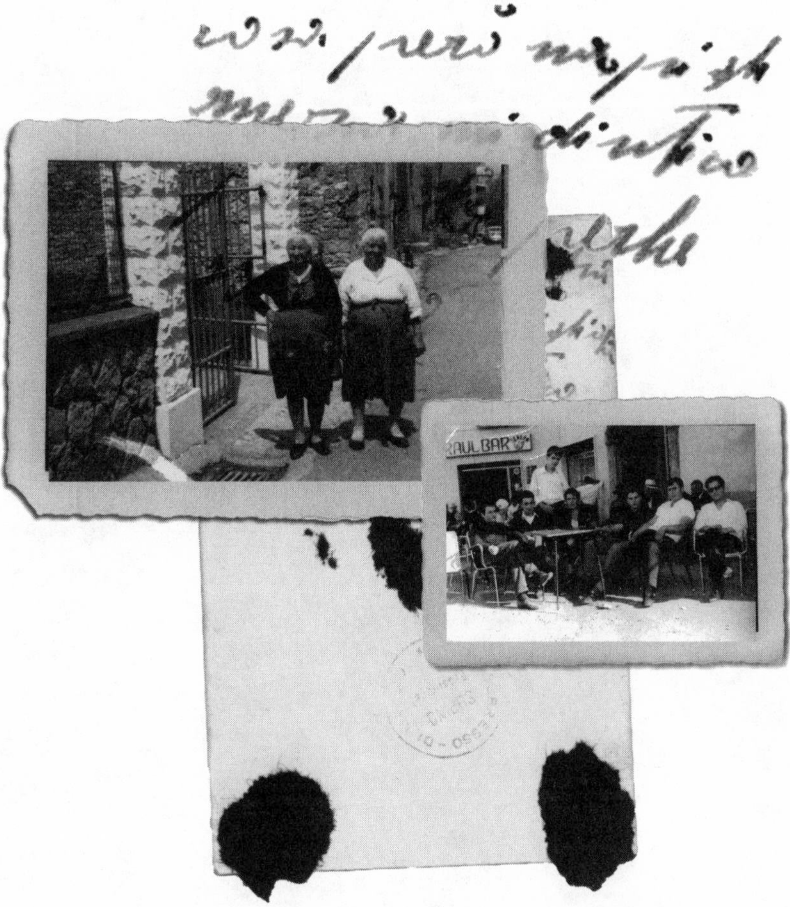
RAUL BAR

Maybe It Needs
a Little Work

In May, Bob and I went to Supino to inspect our new house. We had the address, but first we had to stop at Enzo's house, Raffaele's brother, to get the key. There was a light rain falling when we arrived at Fiumicino Airport. We drove straight from the airport to Supino and knocked on the brother's door just after one o'clock.

"You arrive already. Good. Sit. Eat," said Enzo.

We were too excited to eat, but we didn't want to insult him by refusing his hospitality. Already Enzo's wife was gathering more plates and glasses from the sideboard. I explained to the woman with some hand gestures that we were very tired. I said, "*Un'altra volta*," which I think meant "another time." Covering Enzo's dish of linguine with another plate, she motioned to her husband to take us to the house.

"It's not necessary," said Bob. "*Non é necessario*. You stay and eat your lunch. We have the address. Just give us the key."

"No. No," replied Enzo, shocked by the suggestion. "It is my pleasure, my honour, to show you the house of my brother. Then, I present you with the keys, my new Canadian friends, and we have a drink to celebrate."

Five minutes later, we parked our rented car beside the Bar Italia and ran up Via D'Italia and onto Via Condotto Vecchio. It was raining fairly heavily now and water ran down the gutters of the cobblestone street. The stone houses that lined the street were joined in one long building, so we hurried past several doors until Enzo stepped under an archway. It was a small stone entrance-way, about a yard by a yard, with two sets of stairways, one going left and one going right. The cement work on the left stairway was cracked and broken, but Enzo turned to the right, where the stairs were in excellent condition, and we followed him to the front door of our new home. The double wooden doors had long etched glass panels. Enzo took the key from his jacket pocket and slipped it easily into the lock.

"*Ascolta,*" he said, cupping his hand over his ear. "*Uno, due, tre,*" and we heard three little clicks announcing that the door was unlocked. Enzo stepped aside to allow Bob to enter first, but when Bob pushed on the polished brass door handle, nothing happened. He pushed again. Then, he leaned one arm on the door frame and gave a quick shove with his shoulder. There was a screech as the door scraped an arc onto the dirty cement floor. A foul smell greeted us and sent us reeling back down the stairs and into the street.

"*Un momento, un momento,*" instructed Enzo, as he raced through the house, opening windows and doors. With one hand masking my mouth and nose, I slowly paced the length of the main floor. Sixteen feet by ten feet of cold, damp, dirty floors and clammy walls festooned with crumbling paint chips. In the corner was a fireplace, decorated with dull mustard-yellow and turquoise ceramic tiles. Every tile was cracked or chipped. Some were missing altogether and in their place remained a streaky square of grey grout. On the walls above the fireplace were vertical charcoal streaks where the rainwater had seeped in. Plastered solidly into the cracked ceiling were three large, rusty hooks.

"What are these?" I asked, pointing to the hooks.

"Meat-a hook," Enzo replied, happy to point out this added feature. "For hanging *salsicce* — how you say? — sausage."

As I put my foot on the first step, I thought beneath the dirt there might be marble, but the steps were damp from the rain and I slipped. Reaching out to steady myself on the banister, I watched the whole railing fall slowly to the floor. Bob caught me under my arms. I went up the stairs slowly, balancing myself with one arm extended into the damp, musty air, the other pressed against the stairwell. As I climbed, bits of plaster crumbled beneath my fingers and trickled down the wall. With each step, I hoped for reassurance that the upstairs might be in better condition. The stairs ended where the front bedroom began. Its balcony doors were open and the wind carried the rain into the room. Water also overflowed a small pothole in the balcony floor, travelling along a crack and into the bedroom where it collected in a puddle around my feet.

"I think the air is fresher up here," I said. "And when

the sun comes out — the sun will come out eventually, won't it? — that breeze will be refreshing, right? Bob? Right?"

"Let's look at the third room," Bob said.

The floor was dry and a little larger; it would likely accommodate a double bed. I opened the closet door to a tiny window. If we took out the broken toilet and wash basin someone had stored in there and added a clothes rod, this could be a handy little addition. It even had a light switch, but when I switched it on, nothing happened. Looking up to see if the bulb was burned out, I saw a rusted shower head in the middle of the ceiling.

Enzo squeezed between the cracked toilet bowl and the grubby sink and with a flourish turned on the tap. A few hearty sputters of protest and copper-coloured liquid spurted from the tap, for a moment. Enzo explained that we had town water access for an hour each day. On our street, Via Condotto Vecchio, we could usually get water from the taps between eleven o'clock and noon, most days.

"How do people manage the rest of the time?" I asked.

Enzo shrugged. "Fill pots," he said.

Cold water ran from the second tap too, for a few seconds. "Where's the hot water?" I asked.

"You require hot water too?" asked Enzo.

I walked the three steps to the back bedroom window. I was tired from the flight and the rain outside made things seem more dismal. The smell didn't help either. From the balcony at the front of the house, I could see people heading up the hill to get water from the mountain stream, or down the hill to the shops of Supino, but the view from the back bedroom overlooked a ravine. Suddenly, I was in the country. The top half of the cracked glass framed a view of Santa Serena. The bottom half of the glass showed the valley of beech and hazelnut trees, shiny, yellow-green leaves and slender trunks bowing gracefully in the rain. Halfway up the hillside stood the farmhouse where my father was born. I could see the faded, clay tile roof through the spaces in the trees. I could see the farmhouse walls, shiny in the rain, the old wooden gate, the pathway edged with grapevines. I could pick out the three olive trees and the cherry tree that I knew would be in blossom.

"What do you think?" asked Bob.

I couldn't think of one word to say, in English or Italian.

Back on the main floor, Enzo pushed one of the front doors closed and in the wall behind it was another smaller door. He opened it and stood with his hand extended revealing a tiny triangular closet with a slanted roof (created by the stairway), a wooden shelf, smoke-coloured cobwebs and four coat hooks. Enzo reached in and took an enormous key off the shelf. The key was 10 inches long, made of black wrought iron, with an ornate handle of loops and scrolls. A key designed for a castle.

Enzo held the key carefully in both hands and turned to Bob. "*La cantina,*" he said.

That word, *cantina*, wine cellar, made me realize there was no basement in this house. Where *was* the *cantina?* We stepped outside, under the archway that covered our tiny verandah and narrow stairs, and Enzo locked the front door. He presented Bob with the house keys. Bob passed me the *cantina* key, which weighed at least five pounds. If I put this key in my pocket, I'd lean to one side as I walked. I carried it down the stairs in both hands, as if it was treasure, and then I turned to walk down the street to the Bar Italia where we'd parked the car.

"*Aspetta*," said Enzo. "Wait." He pointed to our house. The rain had stopped, but water still dripped through the holes in the eavestrough, down the walls past the rusted balcony railing, around the dingy arch of the verandah and down to the road, where it flowed along the gutter past two wooden doors. Enzo was pointing to these, at street level: double doors of thick oak planks tapered perfectly to fit the cement archway.

"*Questa é la tua cantina*," announced Enzo, looking at me.

I lifted the key into the lock, as large as a dinner plate, and turned with both hands. The oak doors didn't move an inch. Bob pushed on one door, Enzo pushed on the other, I held my breath. A wise move because the same sour smell was just as powerful here. Although the *cantina* may have held barrels and barrels of valuable wine at one time, now it contained nothing but shadows and spider webs. Enzo pulled on a chain and the *cantina* was flooded with light. The walls were perfectly smooth and white. Firewood was piled neatly along one wall, the other walls bare. The ceiling was decorated, not with rusty meat hooks, but with swirls of plaster. The cement floor was swept clean. In the back corner there was a window with vertical iron bars. Even though the *cantina* was not actually *in* the house, it was still the nicest room in the house.

"What do you use this *cantina* for?" asked Bob. "*Perché?*"

Enzo stared at him in disbelief, not because he didn't understand Bob's Italian, but because he couldn't comprehend the question.

"*Vino* — wine," he said, politely, but he shook his head a little. Enzo brightened, waved his hand toward the Bar Italia and invited us to coffee. It was a Supinese tradition to make everything into an occasion, a ceremony. There was a certain prestige involved in bringing North Americans into the Italian coffee bar, especially since these Canadians liked the village so much they'd bought a house. We accepted the offer of coffee, the same way we were going to have to accept a lot of things.

When we arrived at the Bar Italia, Rocco was waiting inside. "Don't tell me," he said. "I can tell by the look on Maria's face. You're disappointed. Maybe it needs a little work."

Enzo carefully hung my knapsack on a hook near the cash register, ordered cappuccino for the *signora*, *biscotti* and espresso for *signor* Bob, and made a little ceremony out of pulling out my chair, sweeping some invisible crumbs from the tabletop. Rocco, not to be outdone, ordered espresso for everyone in the bar. Then came the introductions.

Rocco's brother Pietro was a contractor — we might need to hire him. Every man in the bar turned out to be a relation of Rocco's. They were all involved in the construction trade. We met Rocco's cousin Paolo, the plumber, his brother Vincenzo, the painter, his brother-in-law Luigi, the floor sander, and Rocco's father-in-law, Maurizio the tile man.

After an hour, Bob and I stood up, ready to leave, but Pietro suggested, since it had stopped raining, that we all walk back to the house together and make a list of what needed to be done.

Bob said, and I knew he wasn't kidding this time, "You'll need a long piece of paper."

We left the bar deserted, except for Enzo. Apparently he felt that his job was done. Enzo stayed behind to play cards with Bruno, the owner. We were on our own, with five tradesmen and a travel agent.

Bob unlocked the front door and stepped back to let the tradesmen go in first. It was more than a polite gesture; we didn't want to breathe that stagnant air any longer than we had to. Rocco took the newspaper that he always carried under his arm and crumpled it in the fireplace. He lit it and added thin twigs from a battered metal pail in the corner of the room. In a few minutes, the flames began to throw light and warmth into the room. Bob went down to the *cantina* and returned, carrying two beechnut logs.

Pietro said we must start at the top and work our way down. I thought the stench must be getting to him too, so I assured him the air was fresher upstairs. In the tiny front bedroom, a dingy rope hung from the corner of the ceiling. Why hadn't we noticed it before? Pietro pulled the rope and down came a flight of stairs. Pietro snapped a brass hinge into place, put his foot on the bottom step to steady it and with a sweep of his arm and a formal bow, he said,

"Eccola." We climbed the ladder and found ourselves in a bright and airy attic, bright and airy because several roof tiles were missing. There was blue sky above us in several locations and underneath each opening, a puddle of fresh rainwater.

"Primo," announced Pietro. *"Il tetto nuovo."* A new roof.

"Certo," agreed Rocco.

"Secondo," decided Pietro. *"Imbiancare* — how you say? — paint the walls."

"Certo," replied Rocco.

"Terzo," continued Pietro. *"Le finestre nuove."*

"Certo," said Rocco and so it went until we climbed down the ladder to the little closet that was the bathroom and Rocco's cousin, Paolo the plumber, took over.

"What you like?" he asked. "New toilet — maybe clean up the sink a little?"

"No. Whole new bathroom."

Paolo looked a little unsure. "You mean everything — new toilet, new sink, new shower head?"

"No. Whole new bathroom," I repeated and I took his piece of blue chalk and marked off a corner of the second-floor bedroom. "Make a whole new bathroom and make it this big."

"Mamma mia."

Pietro brought out his list and started adding to it: plaster the cracks, fill in the pot hole on the balcony, paint everything. Vincenzo, the painter, interrupted.

"Colore?" he asked. "I paint light, or dark?"

"Light, *certo,*" responded Rocco and we trooped down

the stairs to the main floor. It was Rocco's brother-in-law's, Luigi's, turn; he sanded floors.

"But these floors are cement," I said.

"No. No," assured Luigi. "Marble. I sand. You see. É *bellissimo.*"

The fire had warmed the room and eliminated some of the smell. The sun was shining through the open door. Rocco's father-in-law, Maurizio, tapped his finger against the grimy yellow tile that decorated the front of the fireplace.

"What you think?" he asked. "Maybe I replace one or two tiles — this one, she's a little cracked."

"*Certo,*" agreed Rocco.

But Bob intervened, "Take them all off — *tutto* — and make a brick fireplace with a wooden mantle."

"Bricks? You want bricks *inside* the house?"

"*Certo,*" said Bob.

Pietro wrote down everything we needed, Rocco translated it for us and we signed at the letter X. Pietro assured us that work would start *presto* and we could stay in the back bedroom in the meantime. There was a bathroom at the Bar Italia, just down the street.

We said we would stay at the local *pensione* while the house was being renovated, confirming the villagers' suspicions that we were *ricchi e pazzi.* Rich and crazy. We were the last ones to leave. I reached into my knapsack and brought out a wreath of grapevines, dried flowers and blue gingham ribbon and hung it on the front door. There was a little hand painted sign in the shape of a heart in the centre of the wreath: "Welcome."

We walked down the cobblestone street to the Bar

Italia where we had parked the car. Things were looking up; the house needed more work than we had thought, but we'd arranged for all the renovations in less than two hours. We could sleep for the rest of the day, at the *pensione* just outside of town, and tomorrow when we returned to the house it would be an Italian beehive of activity.

"I'm feeling better," I began. "This village is...."

"There's a parking ticket on our car," said Bob.

The windshields of the other cars were bare. A trio of young men, lounging in front of the Bar Italia smoking Marlboro cigarettes and reading *Lo Sport*, laughed at us.

"*Milanese*," they shouted, pointing to our licence plate.

"Why are we the only ones with a ticket?" asked Bob, as we got into our rented Fiat.

"No idea. We could ask the policeman who directs the traffic at the corner."

Rocco had told us the village of Supino boasts three policemen: one sometimes directs the cars at the main intersection, the other two are on call for feast days, official visits and parades. Today there wasn't anyone directing traffic at the corner.

"Do you want to stop at the police station?" I asked. "See if we can pay it there?"

"I guess. We're going right by it to get to the *pensione*."

The street seemed unusually busy for this time of day; no one was leaning on the fence posts chatting with their neighbour or napping under the grapevines with their handkerchief draped over their head. The day was still bright, yet herds of sheep crowded the road leading to the outskirts of town. The sign on the police station stated: OPEN: 16:00–20:00.

As we pulled into the driveway, a uniformed officer raced out and shooed us away with his white hat. "*No. No. Calcio,*" he yelled.

In his haste to close the wrought iron gates he scraped the front fender of the car. Bob had learned *some* Italian mannerisms. He blasted the horn, shook his fist at the policeman. He pointed to his watch and then to the sign.

"*Calcio,*" repeated the officer. Kicking his foot in the air, he wagged his index finger at us. "*No. Assolutamente, no.*"

At the *pensione*, the coffee grinder on the black marble bar whirred as it pulverized the beans for espresso. Ugo the waiter stood at the dining room door anxious to seat guests. It was six o'clock. We knew dinner was never served before eight.

"What's going on?" I asked Ugo. "*Che é successo?*"

"*Calcio,*" he explained. "Foota-ball."

"Soccer," translated Bob.

Remembering the busy streets, the traffic jam of sheep, I realized the villagers were hurrying home to eat early so they could return to the coffee bars to watch the eight o'clock game.

"Ask him about the parking ticket," said Bob.

"Why us?" I asked Ugo, pointing to myself and then to the ticket.

"Your machine," he explained, "*Milanese.*" Calling to his father, Ugo took our parking ticket and laid it carefully in the palm of his hand. In a few minutes, the entire family had crammed into the lobby to examine the official paper.

Even the chef scurried out of the kitchen, wiping bits of yellow egg dough on his apron. Although everyone crowded close to Ugo, no one actually touched the parking ticket. The grandmother started chattering and waving her hands toward a shelf above the cash register. There was a photo of the town's patron saint, San Lorenzo, and a dried leaf from Palm Sunday that someone had fashioned into a cross. The grandmother made a little space between these treasures and held her hand out for our parking ticket. The father, Ugo Primo, stepped forward with a thumb tack in his hand. He dusted off a small section of the wood paneling behind the bar with his handkerchief. This was where he proudly displayed his postcards from former guests and his picture of the Lazio soccer team. Just as I was beginning to realize that we were not going to get our ticket back, the mention of soccer sent the family hurrying back to work. Ugo hustled us to a table. On his way he grabbed a bottle of *Castelli Romani*, a basket of bread.

"*Mangia presto*," he announced. He was gone before the wine bottle settled onto the white linen tablecloth.

"The cloth's still damp," Bob pointed out. "And why are we eating so early? The table's not even set."

"*Buona sera*," said Rocco, as he rushed into the dining room.

"We haven't ordered yet and Ugo says our food will be here soon," complained Bob.

"There's a soccer game tonight," reminded Rocco, as he pulled over a chair.

"We got a parking ticket," continued Bob.

"Yes. I heard. Let the management keep it."

"Can we pay it without the original?"

"No one pays tickets in Supino," explained Rocco. "Most people have never seen one. The police don't know you're Supinese because your licence plate says Milanese like all Italian rental cars. They figured you're lost tourists."

"Do you mean if they knew we'd just bought a house in Supino they wouldn't have ticketed us?" I asked. "That's very neighbourly."

"It's nothing to do with being neighbourly. If a policeman gave a ticket to a villager, they'd be outraged. So would their family. They'd seek revenge."

"What revenge? They'd have to pay, wouldn't they?"

"Sure they'd pay. But the policeman would pay too," Rocco assured us. "One day one of the policeman's chickens would go missing, or a bushel of grapes would disappear."

"But the police would know who took it. It wouldn't be worth a stolen chicken or a few grapes — everyone in Supino has those things anyway."

"That's not the point. The villagers would be insulted by the betrayal of one of their own."

"Even so, the police know the guilty party, or at least the guilty family."

"The villager's friends would get involved. It's a small village. The policeman's probably related to the family through blood, or marriage, or...."

"Ahhh, our fettuccine is here," announced Rocco, as Ugo arrived carrying three plates. Apparently Rocco was eating dinner with us.

"*Buon appetito.*" Lifting his wine glass in a toast, Rocco said, "Welcome to Supino."

We were too tired to sit in the bar and watch the soccer game with the rest of the villagers. We worked our way through the crowd and the smoke, heading for our bedroom on the second floor. Beside the elevator was a six-sided rack on a swivel base, filled with postcards. One card showed an aerial view of the village, lying peacefully in the valley under the shadow of the Santa Serena mountain. Another was of the war memorial in the main square, built in the 1950s. The last was a view of the main street with the Kennedy Bar in the corner.

"*Buon giorno*," we said to the town official, seated at the desk, reading *Il Tempo*.

"*Un momento*," he replied, without looking up.

Several *momentos* passed before he folded his newspaper, straightened his tie and removed his uniform jacket from the back of the chair. We placed our letter of purchase, our passports and our "official request to install a water tank" on the desk and waited. This was our fourth trip to City Hall. The first time, we'd received the official form, but when we'd returned the next day, City Hall was closed for lunch, for three hours. We came back again after lunch, but they were still closed. Then on Saturday, and Sunday, and Monday, but the doors were still locked.

"Maybe they're closed on Monday," I said to Bob, but really I had no idea why the doors were locked. We'd been in Supino for six days now and all we'd accomplished was signing the renovation contract.

The City Hall employee stood up, put on his uniform jacket and left the room. In a few minutes, we heard the front door open and close, followed by the sound of whistling. We rushed to the open window just in time to see our man strolling down the street, whistling happily, heading to the Bar Centrale.

"Darn," groaned Bob. "It's ten o'clock. Cappuccino break."

We walked down to the Bar Centrale too. Our town official was arguing politics with some friends at a nearby table. Every few minutes he banged his hand emphatically on the metal table top, the glasses rattled, the cups clanked, but the conversation carried on. Rocco came whistling up the street, newspaper under his arm. He veered off as soon as he saw us and pulled a chair up to the table.

"How are you making out with the lawyer?" Bob asked.

"Which lawyer is that, Bob?" replied Rocco, as he signalled to the waiter, waved to a friend whizzing by on a motor scooter.

"The lawyer who's supposed to register the deed of our house."

"Oh, yes, of course. There's no lawyer in Supino, you understand, Bob," Rocco explained. "We'll go to Frosinone."

"Not enough work for a lawyer here?" asked Bob.

"The Supinese don't trust lawyers. They think they're thieves — charging for advice you could get free at any bar in town."

"Don't they appreciate the educational costs, the time involved in becoming a lawyer?"

"Time. That reminds me," Rocco replied, looking at his watch. "Be in Frosinone tomorrow, Via Margerite #7, at one o'clock. We have an appointment."

The Supinese have a different concept of time. They say one o'clock, but they show up two hours later.

"Do you mean one o'clock? Sharp?" I asked.

"*Sí. Sí,*" Rocco nodded, then sighed. "That's the other reason a lawyer can't practice here. The Supinese are suspicious of people who are obsessed with time."

That morning in the *piazza* the sun was strong. Our town official took off his jacket. Since I didn't think he'd be returning to City Hall soon, we left the Bar Centrale and walked down the hill to the Kennedy Bar where they sold ice cream: lemon to pucker your mouth, hazelnut to sharpen your taste buds and peach to seduce you. We sat at a small white table beneath the shade of a quince tree and watched a city employee plaster a yellow poster to the side of the bar. When he finished he came over to speak to Bob.

"*Caffé?*" asked my husband.

"*Sí. Grazie,*" replied the stranger.

Bob signaled the waiter, held up his thumb and index finger to indicate two.

"Who is this man?" I asked.

"It's the street sweeper. You see him every morning at the Bar Italia, leaning on his broom, talking to the policeman who sometimes directs the traffic."

The three of us sat comfortably in the eleven o'clock sunshine, drinking espresso, exchanging a word or two. With my glasses and my dictionary, I translated the poster.

It was an announcement of the activities surrounding the feast of San Cataldo. We'd been invited to participate in the official ceremonies at City Hall. I thought it was because my husband was a politician. The villagers love titles: *professore*, *dottore*, *consigliere*, especially if it's a local made good. Partway through my translation I discovered a line in English.

"Bob, listen to this. Official visit of *signor* Robert McLean, Alderman City of York (Toronto) four o'clock Tuesday, May 8th at City Hall. That's today," I said. "What time is it?"

"Eleven. We've got lots of time. Four o'clock in Supino probably means six."

Before heading back to the *pensione* to change, we stopped again at the Bar Centrale. Our city official had removed his tie, loosened his collar, rolled up his sleeves and was still deep in conversation. We knew there was no way he was going to return to his duties at City Hall today. The ten o'clock cappuccino break had stretched almost to lunch time. We carried on up the hill to our house to see how the renovations were progressing. The workers were also on a break, sitting beneath the willow tree in the empty lot up the road, drinking beer and eating cake, supplied by *signora* Francesca who lived across the street. They jumped up when they saw us approach. Not to work, but to tell us Gino's brother had just returned from Toronto with pictures of the CN Tower.

"Isn't it strange how fascinated the villagers are with the CN Tower?" I asked.

"Isn't it strange that no one's working?" responded Bob.

Our house was locked, tools, paint cans, plaster neatly piled in the *cantina*. The workers gathered up their sweaters and their caps and headed home.

"See you later," they claimed. *"Ci vediamo."*

"They accomplish a lot when they're working," I said.

"Sure," agreed Bob, *"when* they're working. They stop for the strangest reasons. What about last week? The whole town shut down to hike up the mountain for an afternoon picnic. And why? Because the wild roses were in bloom or the cherries were ripe. What kind of a village is this anyway?"

"My father's village," I replied.

We passed the house again, just before four, en route to the official ceremonies. I assured Bob we'd see workers in action. The street was deserted. We drove to City Hall without passing a single car or person. The doors of the municipal building were locked.

"We'll try the Bar Centrale," suggested Bob. "Maybe the owner, Carlo, knows something."

The *piazza* was empty. The bar was closed. Even our town official had gone.

"Interesting way to hold an official opening."

"Let's go sit on our balcony," I replied. "I think the workers will be back from their lunch break soon."

On our narrow balcony two cane chairs, left in the attic, fit side by side, but we had to climb over their wooden ladder backs to sit down. There was nowhere to put our legs. For a few minutes, we sat folded like jackknives, until we traded the chairs for empty plaster pails. Perfect. From up the mountain, a soft thumping noise grew louder, approached the curve of our street. As we turned toward the sound, a brass band appeared around the bend, horns shining in the sunlight, drums beating brightly. When the band passed the houses along Via Condotto Vecchio, the villagers spilled from their doorways. Dressed in their Sunday clothes, mothers pushed strollers, children skipped, men straightened their ties and their collar bands; the street joined in a parade. When they passed our balcony, we deserted our plastic pails and joined as well.

Down the hill we proceeded, gathering neighbours as we went, past the Bar Centrale, still closed, and up the hill to the City Hall where red and yellow banners fluttered from its second story windows. The doors stood wide open with a uniformed policeman at each end. The crowd gathered outside the doorway and waited. Another policeman stepped out. He held a bugle to his lips and played a few notes.

"This must be something really important. All three Supino policemen are here."

Dignitaries in black suits filed out of the building. The last man wore a red, white and green sash tied diagonally across his chest. The mayor made a fine speech about something, speaking so quickly I couldn't decipher enough words to create a sentence. Then he spoke in English, "*Signor* Bob, welcome. Missus Bob, welcome home." The mayor placed a bunch of red roses in my arm, shook my hand and kissed me on both cheeks. Even though it was my father's birthplace, my father's country, my father's language, it was the moment I felt *I* belonged.

❖

The next day, as we drove down Via Condotto Vecchio, Bob checked the gas gauge. It was almost empty.

"Is there a gas station in Supino?" he asked.

"Isn't there one near the Kennedy Bar?"

"You're thinking of the phone booth. I'd better stop and ask. I don't think we have enough gas to get to Frosinone."

Attached to the Kennedy Bar is a pizza parlor. The woman who makes the pizza doesn't speak English, but she has a pleasant face and like all the Supinese, she's anxious to help. We can look up the phrase "gas station" in the dictionary and ask her. That's the easy part. The hard part is the answer. Someone always has a better way of getting there and every heated conversation always ends with the question, "Understand?"

Bob memorized the words for "right" and "left," copied down the words for "where," and "gas station" and was back to the car in a few seconds.

"That was almost too fast," I worried. "What'd she say?"

"Quattro Strade — the four streets, we know where that is. Turn right and boom! That's it."

So we drove with Bob watching the gas gauge all the way and turned right and boom! There it was. We waited in the car for a few minutes, Bob tapping his fingernails on the dashboard, but no one came. Bob suggested, "Maybe it's self-serve."

"I don't think I've ever seen the word 'self-serve' in Italy," I said, but no one was coming and we had to be in Frosinone in 20 minutes. Bob opened the car door and stepped up to the pump. He squeezed the gas pump, but nothing came out.

"*Ey!*" called a voice from the window above the gas station. "What you do?"

Bob began a pantomime, holding up the pump, pointing to the car, asking me, "What's the word for empty?"

"Come back Thursday," said the man in the window. "I get gas on Thursday."

"You have no gas?" asked Bob. "You're out of gas?"

"Just until Thursday," the man repeated. "Come back Thursday."

"I have to get to Frosinone, today," explained Bob.

"You got *some* gas?" asked the man, sticking his hands out the window and lifting them up and down, as if he was comparing some invisible weights.

"Yes."

"Then, you got no problem, *signor*. You *Americano*?"

"*Canadese*," said Bob wearily, as he screwed the gas cap back on the car's almost empty gas tank.

"Oh, the *Canadese*. To Frosinone, go straight," instructed the gas man. "Why you look so worried? It's all down the hill from here."

We drove down hill until we got almost to the *autostrada*. Before the car could begin to cough and sputter and announce it was completely out of gas, I pointed to a battered blue tin sign, stating *chiuso*, hanging on a chain across the gas pumps. A young boy on a two-wheeler came racing out of nowhere and braked in a spin beside Bob's window.

"*Signor Canadese?*" asked the boy.

"*Sí.*"

"*Aspetta,*" the boy replied, as he reached into his pocket and pulled out a ring of keys. Quickly, he unlocked the chain, unhooked the gas pump and filled the tank. He pointed to the total showing on the gas pump and put his hand out to Bob. Bob counted out the lire, asking, "How did you know who we were?"

"*Telefona,*" he said, pressing his thumb to his ear, his baby finger on his lower lip. "*Canadese.* No gas. Frosinone."

"The guy at the other station must have phoned ahead," I said to Bob.

"*Supinese,*" the boy explained. "Like you."

Bob drove like an Italian maniac all the way to Frosinone. We got there with 10 minutes to spare.

"Bet we're waiting here for over an hour," I said to Bob.

"Not a chance. Lawyers are the same everywhere. Time is money."

There was something about the traffic, the people, even the heat of this small city just 30 minutes from Supino that suggested business and industry. Rocco pulled up five minutes before noon, jumped from his car, raced to the building. It was the fastest we'd ever seen him move. By the time we reached the front lobby Rocco was already at the top of the stairs. He motioned us to hurry.

"Number 27. This is it," said Rocco. "Good luck."

"Aren't you coming with us?" I asked.

"No need. You have your papers, right? Everything's all set. No problem," assured Rocco. Then, he added, "Don't worry, Maria, the lawyer speaks perfect English."

"We've heard that before," I declared, but Rocco was

gone with a wave of his hand and a *"Ciao, bella."*

After the midday heat of Via Margarete, the lawyer's office, with grey marble floors and rich green plants, was cool and peaceful. The receptionist looked up for a moment when we entered and waved us toward the open door of the lawyer's office. No *buon giorno*. No handshake. Not even an enquiry. The lawyer, in his Armani suit and Versace tie, was just as businesslike.

"Sit," he instructed. We pulled out the soft leather seats and sat.

"Sign here," he said.

"These are the same papers we signed at the lawyer's office in Toronto," began Bob. "Why do we have to sign them again?"

"This is Italy," the lawyer replied, so we took the fine-tip fountain pen and signed.

The lawyer placed a small wooden box on the table, opened the lid and from a bed of burgundy velvet, took out a block of dark blue sealing wax and a metal seal. With his cigarette lighter, burnished silver with his initials discreetly engraved in the bottom-left-hand corner, he lit the wick and dripped wax onto the official documents. Then he pressed the seal down firmly on the melted wax and waited a few seconds, tapping his manicured fingertips on the mahogany table. Lifting the seal he said, "You are now official residents of Supino. *Auguri*. Any questions?"

"Our water tank," began Bob.

"Municipal business. Go to the City Hall in your village."

"Our house has several different numbers painted on it," Bob explained. "Six. Ten."

"Ask your neighbours."

He checked his Rolex watch. "Anything else?" he asked and stood up to indicate that the appointment was over. He walked over to the sideboard. A bottle of amber-coloured liquid and several glasses waited on a silver tray. Were we going to drink a toast to our official status? He returned with one last document, opened the folder carefully, turned the paper toward us and, keeping his hand outstretched, waited.

"And this is?" Bob asked.

"My bill," said the lawyer, in his perfect English.

We were out on the street before Bob spoke again. "It's 253,000 lire. That's $253 for who knows what? Advice that you could get for free at any bar in town."

We took the shortcut back to Supino. It's a shorter trip if you avoid the rush hour when the sheep, walking 12 abreast, jam the roadway between the green pastures, ripe with clover and the stone building at the rear of the shepherd's home. It was hot. Beneath the chestnut and fig trees that dotted the countryside, instead of the usual dark patches of shade, circles of white woolly mounds rested in the shadows. We drove along the bridge, built with wooden planks and low rocks, around the bend by the ancient chestnut tree and onto the smooth paved road that runs parallel to the *autostrada*. Bob slowed the car and pulled over.

"What's wrong?"

"Let's get out for a minute. I want to show you something." We stood at the side of the road, the sun beating strongly on our shoulders. "You know how the village's two main streets intersect like a cross? Even though you can't see your father's farmhouse because of the trees, if you imagine a body lying on the frame of the cross, his home is at the heart of Supino."

We were anxious to get back to our balcony, to buy sandwiches at the *porchetta* stand near the *autostrada*. We laughed at the crooked blue sign with its arrow pointing upwards and the white letters that spelled: Supino. This was the spot where some kind of magic always began to take hold. We roared up the narrow street, sounded the horn as we entered the one-lane bridge under the *piazza* Umberto, swerved round the quince tree and the two shoe store ladies who were always sitting beneath it crocheting. We zigzagged past the Bar Italia, up the mountainside to Via Condotto Vecchio and home.

"Here's the plan," I said to Bob. "Tomorrow we'll go back to City Hall — well before the ten o'clock cappuccino break — and arrange for a water tank, a hydro meter and an official street number."

"You're #10," said a voice from below, a voice that spoke English. We looked down and saw a short, white-haired man.

"What you eat? Sand-a-wich?" asked the man. "That's no good. Come. The wife — she feed you."

Bob looked at me and said, "What do you...?" but I was already heading for the stairs. I'd seen the stranger's watery blue eyes, his shy and gentle smile.

"My name, Giuseppe. Call me Joe. I been working in

Frosinone. The wife she tells me you were arrived. You, *famiglia Mezzabotte*, no?"

We could smell roasted chicken, with rosemary and garlic, from the kitchen window of Joe's house. Bob would have said he was related to anyone just to get a taste of that chicken.

Joe hustled us into the house, calling to his wife as we entered, "Angela! The neighbours — they sit alone on the balcony. What's a matter with everybody? Where's Marco? Why you didn't call them over, introduce them to your mother, practise to speak the English to them? Sit. Sit. Angela you gonna let these people eat buns. No pasta? No wine? What's a matter with everybody?"

Bob was eating his third piece of roasted chicken when he broached the subject of the water tank.

"Joe we need a water tank for our house. We can put it in the *cantina*. I understand I have to fill out an official form, apply to City Hall."

"I get the tank for you this afternoon, Bob. We go after lunch."

"I don't think City Hall opens until four o'clock. Even then, it doesn't seem to be a definite thing. Sometimes they don't open at all and...."

"Angela. What you call Bruno's cousin? You know, the one who likes to wear the uniform, sit at the desk, read the newspaper."

"Luigi."

"*Sí. Sí.* Luigi. Today's Wednesday. He's at the Bar Italia. Plays cards. We go after lunch. You and me Bob. You brought some coffee from Canada, right?"

"Yes, but how did you...?"

"You're in the coffee business, no? Sixteen employees. Four delivery trucks. And you drive a good car, Lincoln Continental, right? Everybody knows. You bring some coffee for Luigi. He make the papers for you."

❖

It was almost dark when Bob returned to the *pensione*, face flushed, laughing and talking so quickly I could barely understand him.

"Where have you been all this time?" I asked. "Stop waving your hands all over the place. I can't listen and follow your hand gestures at the same time. Do you want some coffee?"

"Please. I already drank four, no five, espressos, none of which I paid for. These *paesani* of your father's! They all talk at once. Faster than I can translate. They fight over who's paying for my coffee. I thought they were going to come to blows at one point. And they expect me to know every relative that ever emigrated from Supino to Toronto. But wait until you hear this."

"What's the house number situation?"

"The house is #10, just like Joe said. Here's how it works: after the First World War, they numbered all the houses in order, then after the Second, so many buildings were abandoned, deserted, they renumbered, but just the houses where people were living. Are you still with me? The empty houses had no numbers. Every decade, they repaint the numbers. Our house has been empty for 15 years, so no need for a number, right? But now that we've bought it, more renumbering. We're #10."

"Who told you all this?"

"Joe, of course. Who else? There's more. The water tank's coming. Just like he said. Two pounds of Canadian espresso coffee, one water tank."

"How did you arrange that without going to City Hall?"

"No idea. Joe did it all. I just handed over the coffee when he told me to. And get this, Joe says the empty place next door to ours has been sold — the backyard too. The new owner — his name's Sam — wants to buy our wood-shed. We talked it over at the bar. Well, mostly the neighbours argued with Joe about how to handle the sale."

"We're going to sell our woodshed?"

"No. Joe's going to fix it up. He said he'll put on a new roof. Everyone here has pleasant memories of your father's family, they call them *famiglia Mezzabotte*. They all have a story to tell about your grandparents, your father, Aunt Regina. They want to watch out for us, make sure no one cheats us, because they think we're rich. We just bought a house, without seeing it, because it's in your father's village. We're spending as much on renovations as we did to buy the house in the first place. We're flying back and forth to Italy twice a year. We rent a car while we're here — half the people who live here don't even own a car. We stay at the *pensione*. We're buying furniture, as soon as we find the furniture store. Face it. By their standards, we can only be *ricchi o pazzi*. Take your pick.

"So, Joe fixes the roof of the woodshed, not because we're using it, not because the roof's leaking, but because it makes it look like we're using it and taking care of it, like the woodshed is important to us. We own the woodshed, even though it's attached to Sam's house next door, but we don't own the backyard to our house, right?"

"Right. Except that never did make any sense to me."

"Joe explained that to me too. Years ago all the houses on our side of the street that are attached, four or five of them including ours, used to belong to one family. They had a lot of children. When the parents died, they divided the house into a series of little houses so that each of the children would have an equal share — three rooms for one daughter, two rooms and a *cantina* for another, two rooms and the woodshed for another. That's how the empty house next door got the backyard and our house got the woodshed that's attached to the empty house."

"Do we own the land that the woodshed's on?" I asked hopefully.

"Joe says no. But — here's the good part — the woodshed stands between Sam's empty house next door and *signor* Mario's woodlot, right? The only way into the backyard of the empty house is the few inches between the woodshed and *signor* Mario's fence. That's okay if you want to walk into the backyard. But say you want to take a wheelbarrow, a backhoe, or a very small dump truck back there. You can't do it. The woodshed blocks the way."

"Sam could drive around our woodshed, through *signor* Mario's woodlot and get into his yard that way."

"No. He can't," explained Bob. "Joe says *signor* Mario won't let him."

"*Signor* Mario's the sweetest guy. He's always giving me a rose from his garden, some rosemary from the bush.

Why wouldn't he let Sam drive through his empty woodlot to get into his backyard and do his renovations?"

"In Supino, a house is no good without land. Where are you going to plant tomatoes, grow grapes, roses, maybe an olive tree? If *signor* Mario won't let Sam drive on his woodlot, Sam will have to find another way to get into his backyard. The only other way is to knock down the wood-shed. Then, he'll have a good wide path to drive his backhoe and dump truck and.... Joe told him we might want some land behind our house. Said he'd try to convince us to trade the woodshed for a piece of property behind our house."

"You mean we're going to get a backyard?"

"*Posso,*" replied Bob.

The ravine behind the house is a field of buttercups. Tall, slender wildflowers nod elegantly to each other, chatting in the early morning breeze. Down the hill a little, the poppies raise their heads. Yesterday they were dark, heavy droplets bent low on slender furry stems, but today their heads are held high reflecting golden sunlight.

"There's a bunch of people in front of the *cantina*," called Bob, from the front bedroom. "What do they want?"

"No idea. Ask Joe. He speaks English."

Joe reminded me of my father. His answers were always simple, direct, but with a hint of disbelief. Like my father, he was patient. The balcony doors in the front bedroom were open. I could hear Bob speaking to Joe in the narrow street.

"Joe. Who are all those people in front of our *cantina*?"

"The neighbours. They wait."

"Wait for what?"

"It's Friday."

"What happens on Friday?"

"Bob. What's the matter with you? The new water tank comes today, no?"

In half an hour, we hear the rumbling of the city truck travelling the new road that circles the ravine as it curves past the water fountain and rambles down the hill to the top of our street. *Signor* Mario's empty woodlot is two doors away from our house and that's where the truck stops. As the driver reaches for the door handle, the crowd of neighbours surrounding the truck are already inspecting and commenting. Everyone discusses the tank's beauty; the colour, not blue but *azzurro*, is *bellissimo*. They are accustomed to using town water for an hour or two each day, so the real beauty is the *size* of the storage tank. "*Magnifico*," they declare.

The shape, stout and low to the ground, becomes a joke, "*Come Mezzabotte*," they say to me. "Like your father."

Mezzabotte is a Supinese family nickname. It means half a barrel, like the shape of my father. It was true, but the family of *Mezzabotte* never knew such luxury; they carried their water from the mountain stream.

As the driver tries to unload the water tank from the truck, Joe shouts orders, "Peppe, Sam. Lift the tank down to Marco and Angelo. Antonio, get out of the way. Let the men do it. Antonio, hold the *cantina* door open. Okay. Get Luigi to help you. Get this dog out of the way. Wait. Wait.

What are you saying? No. We can't put the water tank there. Just a minute. Who's blowing that horn? Who? *Il postino.* Tell the postman he has to wait same as everybody else. *Mmm beh!* Is it my fault he's early today? *Tomei. Chi Tomei?* Tell him they just moved into the third floor, above the *tabacchi* store. Ring the bell. I know the bell says *Volpone.* So what? It's *Tomei.* It's Mario's niece. She married the engineer from Frosinone. I don't know how long. Get your car out of the way, then we can move the truck. This is an official city truck. You think he's going to move for you? I got no time to talk to you. Where's Luigi? Don't leave the tank there. No good. No good, I said. It's got to go in the corner."

Joe says we must put the water tank in the back corner in order to leave room for the wood storage and the conversion of the *cantina* to a garage, for our *macchina.*

"*Macchina?* What *macchina?*" I ask, but no one answers. "Bob. What car?" Bob shrugs his shoulders, palms upwards, with a look on his face that says, "How would I know?"

I sit on the stoop of Joe's house with Angela and watch them unload the water tank. When they finish, the city truck rumbles down the street and the postman slings his leather satchel over his shoulder and zigzags his way up the hill, whistling and slipping letters into mail slots as he goes.

I hear applause coming from my *cantina* and Angela stands up, saying, "They're finished. *Bravo.* I make the coffee."

The neighbours head to Joe's garage, laughing and

talking. I see Bob in the crowd. Someone pats him on the shoulder and says, "Good, Bob." I see Joe's brother, Benito, smile and give Bob the thumbs up sign. Even Benito, who can neither speak nor hear, knows what is going on and I am left to wonder what new decision has been made without me.

Joe stops at the doorway and says, "What's the matter Maria? Why you don't come for coffee? You want to see where we put the water tank, first?"

"No. I'm sure you picked a good place for the tank, I was just...."

"Good place? The only place. Back corner, under the window. You see, Maria, in that way, we leave room for the woodpile and in the middle..." and here Joe paused to get the full effect, "space for the Fiat!"

"Fiat?" I shout. "What Fiat?"

"Doesn't have to be a Fiat, Maria, if you don't want," suggests Joe. "Any small car will fit in that space. It is *perfetto*." And then he is gone.

Everyone has espresso and *biscotti* in Joe's garage. Soon the speed of conversation becomes too fast for me. By the time I translate one word, the speaker is five sentences ahead of me. I go back and sit on the front stoop beside Angela.

"I had a dishwasher once," she says.

The first time Angela left the village, she was 19. Her parents sent her to Toronto to visit her aunt. In Toronto many people who had been born in Supino, or whose parents had been born there, came to the aunt's house to greet Angela and hear the news of the village. Joe had been one of the visitors, but a reluctant one. Joe was on his way to a party at a friend's house and said he'd just drop in to appease his mother and be on his way. He never made it to the party. Three weeks later, Angela and Joe were engaged and by Christmas they were married. Joe had a good job working construction. They bought a bungalow near St. Clair and Dufferin and filled it with furniture and wedding gifts from the villagers. Joe bought a dishwasher. Angela cut out a picture of the dishwasher from the Eaton's catalogue and sent it to her mother in Supino who stuck the picture up in the Bar Italia so everyone could see it. The picture hung there for years, until the sun turned the newsprint yellow. Even then the villagers talked about the white, shiny machine that washed dishes automatically. *"Mamma mia,"* they said. *"Automatico!"* They also had a colour television with a 26-inch screen and every afternoon Angela watched soap operas to learn to speak English. After nine years they had a son and a daughter and a good life.

Then came a letter from Joe's mother saying she was getting old and tired, the house too big — too many stairs and too much work. She was worried about Benito, Joe's brother who had a good job at the post office, sorting mail. He never missed a day of work, never missed mass on Sunday, but Benito was deaf and spoke with his hands. Joe's mother worried that she and the priest were the only two in the village who understood him and both of them were getting old. Who would care for him, speak to him? It was time to come home, live in the house, take care of Benito. Angela and Joe packed up their belongings and shipped them back to Supino. The colour television and the dishwasher were given to her aunt. When they arrived in Italy Angela said, "Even after flying into the night and out of the morning and landing with a bump at Leonardo da Vinci *aeroporto*, I was still crying. I didn't want to leave Canada."

Joe had returned to the garden to pick the endive flourishing after the recent rain. I had heard their story, now I wanted him to hear mine. I told him I didn't want to buy a car now; the house was expensive enough. I wanted to wait.

"You spend money to *rent* a car, but you don't want to *buy* one? Maria, what's a matter with you? Why you want to give money to some rental guy in Roma, every time you come? Those guys — all thieves. Anyway, we gotta buy. We got nothing to trade, except the *cantina*, but then, where you going to park the car?"

My father had always encouraged me to buy rather than rent, own something rather than "throwing money out the window." I was undecided. The neighbours were discussing who would be in charge of the car when we were away. Everyone had a lead and a price: 1,000 Italian lire was worth a Canadian dollar, so everything sounded expensive — the figures were in the millions. I kept saying to Bob, "How much is that? How much is that?" but he just shrugged and walked back to our house, shaking his head.

We were employing half the town, but not much work had been done. Although I appreciated the friendliness of workers and villagers, I wished they'd socialize on their own time. Though Joe spoke English, we had language in common but lacked understanding. Joe used Supino reasoning and *that* didn't help me sleep at night.

"We're going back to Toronto soon, Joe," I reminded him. "When we come back in August, with my father, we want to be able to stay in the house."

"Good. I look forward to seeing *Mezzabotte* again. All the old people, they remember your father. His father was *esperto* — what you call it? — expert at pruning the grapes. Every year, Domenico's grapes grow the most. Pretty soon other people ask him to come and trim their vines. Next year, more grapes. All along the road, where your father's farm is, you see the best grapevines in the village. When your grandfather died, nobody knows his secrets, how to cut the branches just right. Some people they cut too much — others not enough — never like Domenico. He was *perfetto*. But your father, he tells you this, no? Lorenzo, down at the bar, he knows. Come. I buy you coffee. Lorenzo, he tells you the story."

Joe and I walked across the street, through Mario's woodlot, to find Bob. He was standing among the crowd of buttercups in our backyard.

"I made a list," Bob began. "The hydro meter, the plasterer, the handyman, the floor-sanding man, the plumber, the carpenter, the painter, the electrician, the...."

"Bob," asked Joe, "you got the contract from Pietro?"
"Yes."
"You signed?"
"Yes."

"He signed?"

"Yes."

"Bob. You got no problem. When you come back in August with *Mezzabotte*, everything, she's fine."

❖

At the Bar Italia, Bob is just finishing helping Bruno set up the tables and chairs on the outdoor patio. The cracked cement square holds four tables and ten chairs. Yesterday, a city truck had delivered planter boxes to different public sites around the village. The planters were full of flowers. But most of the villagers held the same opinion as my father — you can't eat flowers — so the flowers have been replaced. On the counter inside the bar are velvety blue petunias deposited unceremoniously in a recycled milk carton; outside the bar in the planter box on the patio are three small tomato seedlings.

We were arguing about who would pay for the coffees when Pietro came into the bar. I asked him why he and his contractors were all working next door at Sam's house, when we had hired him just last week.

"Maria," responded Pietro patiently, "*Mezzabotte* doesn't arrive until *agosto*. Look on the *calendario*. It's only *maggio*." He added, almost involuntarily, "*Mamma mia*."

Pietro explained that he'd run into a little problem: our attic window was going to look right into Sam's new bedroom. *Problema. Grande problema.* Without exchanging a word, Bob and I knew we were entering into trade number three.

Joe folded his hands on the table, tapped his thumbs

together. "What you going to do?" Joe asked, leaning forward to hear Pietro's answer. "You already said you'll put in the new window glass. Bob sign; you sign. *Problema, Pietro, grande problema.*"

"Fill in the window with *cemento. Perfetto*," declared Pietro. "You don't need two windows, Bob. You already got one window at the back. *Basta.* That's enough, no?"

"I like that little window," claimed Bob.

"*Mamma mia.* I pay you for the damn window," yelled Pietro. "Bruno, bring me *birra. Presto.*" Bruno brought a pitcher of beer with several glasses and some advice for Pietro.

"*Canadese sono ricchi, no?*" Pietro smacked his head with the palm of his hand and said nothing.

"I have a plan," said Joe, as if he had just thought of it while Bruno was getting the beer. "We make a trade. You take out the kitchen window. Cut the wall down to the floor. Put the door for the backyard. In return, Bob gives you permission to fill in that nice little attic window with *cemento.*"

"*Sí. Sí,*" agreed Pietro, who hurriedly pushed his pen and a napkin toward Joe. Joe drew out the deal and we signed at the X.

On the way back to the house, we'd picked up several extra people. There were two men who sat on the bench at the water fountain every day and waited for a stranger to stop at the fountain who thought he or she could get water from it. The men directed the newcomer up the hill, past our house, to the *pisciarello* where the cold water from the mountain stream ran continuously. But today they gave up their chance to give directions and followed us up the hill. Some children, who were playing soccer, stopped their game and joined us. Angela was just coming out of the *tabacchi* store, pasta and cigarettes in hand, so she joined us too. Christina, who owns the store, was left alone leaning in the doorway, so she locked the door and came along as well.

"What if someone wants to buy something?" I asked Joe.

"They wait. Or they come to the house. Maria, why do you worry so much?"

The villagers had mixed opinions about cutting the doorway. They weren't sure about using the door that Joe had found in the woodshed. It wasn't a sturdy outside door with a solid lock and a heavy metal doorknob; it was an inside door with a frosted glass panel and a slender silver door handle. Joe said it would do for now. He had found a better one, a solid wooden outside door with a good sturdy lock, on the house next door to ours. No one was living in the house, but surely eventually somebody would and they would need a door.

"Bob, you buy this house. No cost too much money. We take off the door. She looks good, no? We put it for the backyard. What do you say, Bob?"

"Buy the house? To get a door? Joe, we can just buy a new door."

"What's a matter with you, Bob? Pietro already told you this at the bar. You've got to pay attention. Luigi he makes shutters and doors. Made to measure. Not like

Toronto where you go to Canadian Tire and buy a door. This is Italy. Luigi can make the door for you. Measure nice. Special wood from Abruzzi region. Strong nails imported from Milano. He sands very smooth, even makes the picture on the door. What do you call that? Woodcarving. He puts stain and wax and polish. Nice, nice. But Luigi — he takes a lot a time. Sure, sure. Luigi tells everybody, '*Sono artiste, grande professore.*' Bigga head, that guy. What a thief! If Luigi's going to make the door for you, Bob, you're going to pay a lot of money. It's much better to buy the house. The house, she's little. Just two rooms, one up, one down. Nothing special. But the door — *bellissima*. You and me, Bob, we knock out the wall between the two houses and *presto*, you have a five-room house. What do you say?"

"*Perfetto*," the neighbours said. "*Bravo*."

"*Perfetto*?" I shouted. "To buy a house to get a door? Not *perfetto*. *Pazzo*."

"Is the two-room house for sale?" asked Bob. "There's no sign."

"Sign? Why you want to waste money on a sign? I already tell the owner nobody want that house. It's too little. Who's going to buy a two-room house? It's a no good for nothing. That guy who owns the house — he lets it sit here empty while he pays rent for an apartment in Roma. His mother, she lived in the house 37 years. Now she's dead. The son wants to sell. He doesn't want to live here. Thinks he's a bigga shot, live in Roma. Even when the mother was living, the son never came to visit. Just phone sometimes on Sunday. Better if the guy think that no one wants a two-room house. We get a better price that way. For now we put the door I found."

As the increasing numbers of villagers joining the debate added their voices, the conversations grew louder and faster and we were left out of the argument. The noise level escalated. The discussion switched from using the found door to how to grade the yard. The backyard is about 10 feet long, before it plunges down the ravine, so Sam was going to dig out the earth, starting at the back wall of the house, and push the excess soil down the hill. How many steps did we want from the door down to the yard? The lower Sam dug the earth the more steps we'd need to get into the yard. The more earth Sam dug out, the longer the yard would be. The backhoe was poised, in the narrow driveway, ready to dig.

I walked 10 steps, yelling out the numbers, "*Uno, due, tre... dieci*," and slapped my hand on the wall of the house and shouted, "See this white line? Ten feet. Our house is 10 feet wide, so the backyard is 10 feet wide too." I marched toward the ravine, to where I had stuck the dead tree branch into the earth. I stamped my foot. "Right here. *Dieci e dieci*. That's the yard. *Eccola*."

But *signor* Mario reminded us that we needed a foot or two extra for flowers and Enrico suggested we should build a low wall because the flowers could go in pots and Joe declared, "No flowers, you can't eat flowers." He claimed he was bringing a cutting from his grapevine to grow over a lattice roof he planned to make from branches and twigs and Francesca said no grapevine, it would make too much shade and Angela reminded us we'd be happy to have the shade when August came around and Bob looked at me and shrugged his shoulders and asked, "Lunch?" and we headed down to the restaurant in the woods and no one missed us.During an early lunch at the outdoor restaurant I told Bob my plan for our backyard. "Picture this — red impatiens that I can plant every summer and wild yellow buttercups that will appear each spring and Joe's grapevine, the shade will be good in the summer when we get the afternoon sun, a terracotta patio...."

We timed our return to Via Condotto Vecchio for after two o'clock when we knew everyone would be home, eating pasta and drinking wine. The backhoe still sat in the driveway of Sam's house next door where our woodshed used to be. All was quiet on the street. Bob opened the front door and we were met with a blast of sunlight. Instead of a kitchen window there was monstrous hole in the back wall and a panoramic view of the ravine behind our house. Wall to wall. Bright yellow-green trees, the kind you see only in the early spring before the heat and the dust of summer powder the leaves, anchored in a base of yellow buttercups.

"Good grief," I exclaimed. "Why would they knock out so much of the wall to put in one door?"

Joe's voice, from his garage across the street, answered, "The neighbours — they can't agree. Where you going to put the door? Pietro makes the doorway in the corner. Out of the way there. But Enzo, he thinks right in the centre looks better. So, we make the hole a little bigger. Then Mario says beside the fireplace, in line with the front door, to catch the breeze. It seems like a good idea. Then Angela calls, it's time for lunch, so...."

Guido surprised me one Sunday with a knock on the door and the news that he had moved from Roma to Supino for the summer. I didn't have wine, or coffee, or even a chair to sit on. I dug around in my knapsack, produced a package of cherry Lifesavers and offered him one of those.

"What's this?" he asked sweeping his arm across the area where the back wall used to be.

"New door," explained Bob.

"The hole — she's too big."

Guido held a rectangular cardboard carton whose contents rattled and clinked. It was a light fixture with a long silver chain and the whole apparatus unfolded to three tiers of cut-glass crystals, candle-shaped lightbulbs and silver beads. It was elegant. It was beautiful. It was enormous. We thanked him profusely and then, because Guido wasted no time, he told us he needed a ladder as he was walking out the door, down the stairs, on his way to the *cantina*. Bob followed with the key. The villagers kept wine in their *cantinas*. Ours contained the water tank, a woodpile and some waiting construction supplies. The *cantina* was at street level and there was no space between the door of the *cantina* and the street itself, so if a car was passing, you had to wait a few seconds before you could get the key into the lock and open the door. This has two purposes: it saves you from getting brushed by a car and it gives the neighbours time to come over and see what's going on. Bob unlocked the *cantina* door and Joe came hurrying across the street. After the introductions, Joe and Guido chatted rapidly in Italian, while Bob searched for a ladder.

"Sorry, Guido. No ladder — no *scala*."

"Bob, what's a matter with you?" asked Joe. "The ladder is right there, on top of the woodpile," and he grasped a thick branch of wood in each hand and lifted five sturdy logs strapped to long poles of hardwood.

At the house, Joe propped up the ladder and Guido installed the light fixture. I flicked the switch, but only to show Guido that the hydro was not connected.

"No wall and no *elettricitá*? *Mamma mia*."

Then Guido told Bob he'd found a car for us to buy. I think his exact words were, "*Una macchina* — *perfetta e* cheap-o." Before Bob had a chance to respond, Angela was tapping on the door, carrying a tray with coffee and biscuits. I flipped over the cardboard box to act as a table. Bob brought the two plastic pails from the balcony and the other pail from the backyard. As hosts, we sat on the hard marble steps, with the cardboard table holding the coffee tray in the centre. We laughed and drank and ate together, as happily as if we were sitting at the finest restaurant in Rome.

Bob asked, "How much is the car? *Quanto costa*?"

"Five *millioni* lire."

"Guido," I said, "we're only here five or six weeks of the year. We don't need to spend $5,000 for a car. Most of the time it will just sit in the *cantina*. It doesn't make sense."

But Bob argued, "Look at it this way. Every time we come here we rent a car. It works out to $1,000 a trip — more if we stay longer than two weeks. In a couple of years, we'll have spent $5,000 and we won't have anything to show for it. If we spend $5,000 now we'll have the car for years. Joe can use the car while we're in Canada. It'll be good for the car to have someone drive it now and again. Joe can come and pick us up at the airport. He'd be doing us a favour by driving it."

The car would be a way to pay Joe back for all his help negotiating house renovations. Joe wouldn't take money.

Guido reassured me, "No hurry, Maria. My son doesn't bring the car until *dopo il pranzo* — how do you say? After lunch. *Mia moglie* waits for us. You eat lunch at my house."

The villagers' concept of invitation did not include the idea of choice. There were a few excuses that were acceptable: a wedding, baptism, First Communion, lunch at a mother's or mother-in-law's. But Guido's my only relative in Italy, except for the second cousins who live in the big house beside my father's farm. Guido is my oldest relative in Supino. Guido is my first cousin. Therefore, we were eating lunch at Guido's house today.

Just past the Bar Italia is a flower shop. Usually the store is locked and if you want to buy flowers you go up the hill to the bar, where the owner is playing cards with the man from the dry goods store. But today was Sunday; the store was open. The traditional hostess gift is flowers, a tray of pastries, or a box of chocolates. The stores that sold these items were usually open Sunday morning, because the villagers were definitely going to take a gift when they went to someone's house for Sunday lunch, but they weren't going to spend their money a day before they had to.

The hostess would always object, chastise us for bringing anything at all, but then display the flowers in a big vase that was waiting on the dining room table and show them to every neighbour who dropped in for coffee, every day, for the next week. If I brought candies they'd go into her best crystal bowl and they too would be displayed, usually on the sideboard. After everyone had taken one, they waited on the sideboard for the neighbours to admire and share. If I brought pastries the shopkeeper would have already arranged them on a foil-covered cardboard tray and they'd become part of the dessert.

Today, I chose a pot of yellow flowers that looked like chrysanthemums. I took the pot inside the store to pay for it and the owner said, "No." At first I thought I'd offered the wrong amount of money, but the owner took the money and put the pot of yellow flowers back outside. Then he selected a dozen velvety red roses and several sprigs of baby's breath from a large plastic bucket beside the counter. He slipped the bouquet into clear plastic and tied the whole thing up with a few yards of white crinkle ribbon. He presented it to me, the ribbon hanging down in curls and the flowers upside-down.

I accepted the bouquet and said, "*Grazie.*" The flower man responded with an expression I'd never heard before, and when I translated it, I was glad I hadn't made a fuss. He said, "*Buon pranzo.*" Good lunch. The walk to Guido's house was a long and winding route uphill. We stopped several times to greet neighbours; all the women looked at the bouquet and commented, "*Bella.*"

The front door of the house was propped open with a pot of flowers: yellow *margheritas.* Guido's wife, Luigina, hurried into the yard, kissed us and hustled us toward the house. She clucked at us along the way as if we were a small group of chickens late for dinner. She was a tiny, energetic woman with curly hair. She wore a flowered dress and, of course, an apron. She smelled of tomato sauce, *basilico* and the scent of fresh air and sunshine. In the dining room there was a china cabinet, a big wooden table and many chairs. I gave Luigina the flowers and she crushed a rose petal under her nose and pronounced the bouquet, "*Bellissimo.*"

"*Grazie. Grazie mille,*" she said as she kissed me again. Guido pulled out a crystal vase from under a dining room chair and filled the vase with water. He put the bouquet on the dining room window ledge where they blocked the view. The fragrance of roses, the scent from the egg noodles, the herbs, the spices, the woody red wine: it was indeed *buon pranzo.*

We were sipping espresso, thick and sugary sweet, when a horn tooted. Guido rushed out to open the gate; Luigina hurried into the kitchen to bring out a fresh plate of fettuccine.

I peeked out the dining room window, making a little space between two roses. "Bob. A taxi's here. And there's no one in it."

"It must be Peppe, Guido's son, the one who's bringing our car."

"Yes, but he's driving a taxi. Bob, Guido's son is driving a taxi, not a car, Bob, a taxi. Look at it. See the sign on the roof? It says TAXI and it's yellow. The taxi is yellow, Bob. And look how big it is. Never mind that. Look how old it is. I don't believe it. We're buying a taxi. We're not...."

"*Grazie. Grazie*," said Peppe as he shook Bob's hand. "Thank you from my wife, from my children. Already I have picked a new taxi. I am just waiting for someone to buy this one. And you buy it! Bob, my Canadian cousin. *Perfetto. Grazie. Grazie.*" He stopped to kiss Bob on both cheeks, "You are a good man, a good cousin. *Grazie molto.*"

Guido was taking a silver tray with shot glasses and a bottle of whiskey from the china cabinet. I knew he'd been saving that bottle for a special occasion. I could see it in his smile, in the way he lovingly broke the seal on the whiskey bottle with his thumbnail. Luigina was standing at the table with her hand on her son's shoulder.

"*Auguri*," I said to Bob. "Congratulations. We just bought a taxi."

When we drove the taxi back to the house later that afternoon we were met by Joe and a new set of problems.

"You see this *cantina*, Bob?" asked Joe.

"Of course."

"You see the taxi you bought?"

"Of course."

"You see a problem, Bob? *Grande problema*?"

"The car won't fit in the *cantina*?"

"Of course."

"We just make the door of the *cantina* a little wider," I said confidently.

"Maria. Look at the arch. 1926. This arch is history. You can't knock it out. We have a law in Supino, remember? Bob, you remember the guy who owns the house next door? The two-room house with the good door. That guy — thinks he's a bigga shot. Likes everything big. All show. No sense, that guy. Rents in Roma, when the house he owns in Supino sits empty. *Mamma mia*. He'd buy this car. Only one problem. That guy — he's got no money."

"Joe. That *is* a problem. *Un grande problema*."

"Bob, what's the matter with you? We make a trade. The big shot and me. The empty two-room house *and* the door!" exclaimed Joe.

"Wait a minute. Joe, you can't trade a taxi for a house. That just makes more problems. If you take the door off the little house, Pietro, or someone, has to fill it in with cement. Someone has to knock out the wall between the houses, so we can get back and forth. Then Vincenzo has to paint the place. And the floor will need to be patched. It's crazy — all that work for a house we don't need."

"Why you worry so much, Maria?"

To avoid another thwarted decision Bob and I jumped in the car and drove to Santa Serena, a mountain rooted in Supino, but with its head in the clouds. "Serena" means clear, but to me it also meant serenity, escape. After a few hours basking in its views and sunlight we headed home. Partway down the mountain, a herd of sheep climbed out of the pasture and crowded onto the road. Beside the road was a stone building and a man painting at his easel. He put down his paintbrush and walked to our car.

"Lost?" he asked, looking at the licence plate.

"No," I assured him. "I belong here."

I asked him about his work. Immediately he revived and offered to show us his studio. He painted ceramic wall tiles using the colours of the coast: white sand, blue sky, yellow sun and, sometimes, a splash of red. Propped on the windowsill were samples of his work. I asked if I could buy two.

"Two tiles? I give them to you." The man clicked on the light, wiped a brushstroke on one tile, swirled a circle on the other. The numbers looked like melted sunshine. We arrived home at twilight, but even in the shadows, we could see no more work had been done. We left our two ceramic tiles, wrapped carefully in brown paper in the attic, and drove to the *pensione* to pack for our return trip.

The plain brown paper wrapper held more than our new ceramic house numbers. It represented my faith in our neighbour who speaks English, in the workers who would finish the renovations on our house by August and in my ability to bring my father back to his birthplace. On Santa Serena earlier that day I had prayed to the Saint of Special Favours that I was not asking too much.

Supino - Chiesa S. Nicola

The Saint of Special Favours

As soon as I arrived in Toronto, I went to visit my father at the drop-in centre. While we were away he'd withdrawn even further. He was spending too much time there, alone. He had never really been comfortable there anyway. His English was good enough, but he didn't join in activities. He needed pocket money for the bingo cards and the nickel a game they charged for darts, so I used to put loonies on the bookshelf, reminding him they were there if he wanted anything, but he never used them. I had bought him a deck of Italian cards and put them on the bookshelf too, but no one at the centre knew how to play, except Luigi the janitor, and he was working. Sometimes, at lunch, Luigi would play a couple of hands with him or my daughter Kathryn would have a game, as the centre was close to her high school, but these games were slower because Kathryn was a beginner. He always let her win.

That day he was sitting in the corner, head down, shoulders slumped, pulling at a loose thread on his sweater. The sweater he wore was too big for him despite a dresser full of others, gifts from his children and grand-children. Other seniors sat reading the paper, drinking coffee, and discussing the day's news. My father can't read without his glasses, kept at home in his dresser drawer, and he hadn't been given money for coffee. "He has coffee at home," my mother would say. "Why does he need money to buy coffee?" When I greet him, it takes him a few seconds to remember who I am.

"Can I buy you a coffee?" I ask him.

A moment passes, then he smiles, "Sure. Want a candy?" He reaches into his shirt pocket and pulls out a half roll of cherry Lifesavers. "Kathryn was here today. She came on her lunch hour."

I take a Lifesaver, not because I want it, but because I don't want him to have any left in his pocket when he walks home this afternoon. My mother will tell Kathryn not to give him candy.

"There's a bingo game this afternoon. Three o'clock," he says. "Your aunt Regina used to play bingo. She won a lamp one time. Your mother says, 'Why do you want to waste money on bingo? A nickel a card.'"

I give him money, but I know he'll put the money in his pocket, take it home, give it to my mother. It reminds him of the days when he was working at Toronto Macaroni, bringing home his salary. "Bob booked the tickets for Italy today."

"Did you get one for me?" he asks.

"Of course."

"Don't tell your mother, yet." He reaches for a book on the bookshelf, opens it to the last page, brings out a piece of paper. It's been folded many times. "The nurse who takes my blood pressure told me I need a new passport," he begins as he unfolds the paper. "I walked down to the post office and they gave me the form. I already signed, but it says here I need a passport photo."

"Do you want to get your photo taken now?"

"Might as well," he replies, folding the paper and giving it to me. We walk to the photo shop and wait while the photographer switches on his lights and adjusts his camera lens. My father sits carefully on the edge of the chair, his hands gripping the seat, his head down, his shoulders slumped.

"Look over here," instructs the photographer, "and lift your head up. Where are you travelling to, sir?"

"Supino," says my father as he straightens his shoulders, lifts his head high and his smile is brighter than the flash of the camera.

I'm relieved when Linda says she'd like to come to Supino with us — another person to help with my father so that, taking turns, we might do a little sightseeing on our own. But then Kathryn says she wants to come too.

"We'll be spending a lot of time just sitting outside the Bar Italia, taking in the village lifestyle," I explain, but that doesn't discourage her. So we buy another seat.

It's a hot August day when the limousine picks us up en route to the Toronto airport. My father stretches out in the back seat, enjoying the richness of a luxury car. He's equally impressed with the airport itself, strolling the polished corridors and looking in store windows. We wait outside the candy shop while Kathryn and my father buy bags of jelly beans and gum drops. We change Canadian dollars into Italian lire notes and coins, which my father happily jingles in his pocket while we wait for our flight. He stands by the window looking at the airplanes at the gate loading and refuelling.

"Flight 437. That's us," says Linda. "Are you ready to go?"

"Sure. Might as well," he replies. "If she goes down, she goes down."

Aboard the flight the stewards speak English to us, but instantly switch to Italian when speaking to my father. He watches the safety video carefully then turns to me, lifts his eyebrows and shrugs. Bob had called Joe last week to tell him the date of our arrival. Joe would tell Angela and later, when she walked to the *tabacchi* store, she'd tell Christina. From there, the man who delivered the ice cream to the shops in the village would transport the news to the Kennedy Bar. It would be the cheese lady, balancing a sturdy wicker basket of bocconcini and ricotta on her head, who would carry the news to the oldest part of the village, where people gather in narrow passageways crowded with pots of azaleas and *basilico*.

But here on the plane, thousands of miles across the Atlantic, my father sits peacefully after dinner, three glasses of burgundy, two black espressos and a sip of cognac, listening to *La Bohéme* and returning to his homeland after 64 years. When he looks up and sees me, he checks his watch, announces, "Only five more hours."

I decide this might be a good time to try to explain how Supino has changed since my father left all those years ago. Change occurs everywhere, except in the memory.

"When we walk down Via Regina Margherita to the Bar Centrale for our morning cappuccino, we pass an old woman with a basket of cheese balanced on her head. She stands in front of a store, just up from the corner where the fish man sets up his table on Friday mornings."

"What store?" asks my father. "There's no store there."

"Things have changed in Supino since you lived there. The store is called Casa Video."

"Was she a short woman, kinda heavy, with a black dress and a white apron?"

"Yes, and a walking stick."

"That's what I thought. That's Angelina. She lives up the mountain near your cousin's place. They have a few sheep. She makes cheese and brings it to town every Friday to sell at the *piazza*."

A few hours later, I hear the airplane window blinds opening, smell the coffee brewing and I open my eyes to the early morning sunlight. My father is still wide awake, watching the sun rise over the Mediterranean Sea, as we begin our descent to Rome's Leonardo da Vinci Airport.

"How are you doing?"

"Good," he says. "Like sitting on the couch watching the television." Then, he reaches into his pocket for his handkerchief, wipes the corner of his eye. "I forgot how beautiful my old country is."

❖

"Is this the road from Rome to Naples?" my father asks. "They paved it. That's good. About halfway — you watch for the sign, Bob — we turn right. That's Supino."

Linda and Kathryn have already succumbed to the warmth of the sunshine and the hum of the motor, both asleep in the back seat. My father sits between them, his eyes like headlights scanning the countryside for his first glimpse of the town of his youth. Bob employs his Italian driving skills and in 45 minutes we're at the Frosinone exit. In a few minutes we turn at the bent and crooked blue sign that announces Supino, past Quattro Strade — and what's this? A new sign, about a yard by a yard, enormous by Supino standards, welcoming us to Supino. My father is nodding his head, turning left to see San Sebastiano and the ancient buildings that line the main street. Except for some new pavement and stoplights, Supino is largely unchanged from my father's view in 1927.

Part way up the hill, Bob slows for the stop light. A policeman shouts, "*Mezzabotte, buon giorno*," as if 64 years have not passed. The officer takes off his hat and waves us ahead despite the red light.

"That must be Luigi, Domenico's son," says my father. "I guess Domenico retired."

We drive under the bridge, past the bakery and the pizzeria, around the shoe store where its owners sit crocheting, a sharp turn at the town clock, past the Bar Italia and up Via D'Italia, toward our house. When we reach the corner where Via D'Italia meets Via Condotto Vecchio, I have my fingers crossed.

The outside of the house has been painted white. Someone has just washed the front steps, droplets of water, pooled in the small holes of the cement stairway, reflect morning sunbeams. Someone has plastered a smooth white archway around the door frame where our ceramic numbers, left in the attic, are mounted: two tiles with blue waves rolling around the edges and in the centre, a splash of red geranium petals. The #10 is painted in sunshine yellow.

I step aside to let Bob unlock the door, but he hands the key to my father who accepts it without question and unlocks the door as easily as if he's lived here all his life. The door swings open and the rank and musty smell is gone. The marble floors are shining, as if they're wet, but the polish is from Luigi's floor sander. *Bellissimo.* The walls are smooth, painted the softest shade of foam with taupe trim. The back wall has been rebuilt and the door hung with brass hinges. Sunlight pours through the bevelled glass panels. I run to the stairway, hurry up the stairs to the front bedroom which has the same coloured walls, the same shiny marble flooring. The balcony doors are bright with paint, the handles sparkling from polish. In the bathroom, white tile, white light, is everywhere. A wild canary sits on the windowsill of the shower stall, splashing in a small puddle and singing.

Suddenly, my father is standing behind me. Outside the window beneath the tall trees grow wild blue chicory flowers and dainty Queen Anne's lace. Rows of olive trees, with silver-grey leaves and small clumps of dark green fruit, grow in tiers. I hear the wind from Santa Serena whispering over the deep ravine below us. The warm summer breeze wafts into our house and wraps itself around us with a soft murmur.

"Do you hear it?" I ask.

"Yes," he says, laughing. "Someone has a new donkey."

"*Buon giorno. Buon giorno*," calls a voice from the street.

"Company?" asks Kathryn. "We've been here three minutes!"

"It's okay. It's Joe, the neighbour who speaks English."

"Well, he's carrying a tray of coffee," says Linda. "I like him already."

We sit on the front steps, in rows, to drink our coffee, but my father is restless, anxious to get moving. He, Bob and Joe go for a walk to Pisciarello, the mountain stream up the hill. Joe and my father balance Bob's blond height with their shorter stature, white hair and woollen vests, walking slowly with a plastic bottle in one hand, the other in their pocket.

I open the back kitchen door, with a little flourish to reveal the garden, soil freshly turned and ready to be planted. If my father were in charge of the garden he would plant lettuce and early spring onions, tomato and pepper plants and zucchini. Soon he'd start wondering if we couldn't keep a few chickens in a pen on the slope that leads down to the ravine and before we knew it, he and Joe would be planting rows of olive trees in tiers on the hillside, devising some sort of net to catch the olives when they ripen and a pulley to haul the bushels of olives up the hill and into the *cantina* for the press. Around the garden is a low concrete block wall and a grey terrazzo patio, not the brick and terracotta I had imagined.

In the attic, Kathryn's new bedroom, the walls are white plaster and the ceiling is made of pine planks coated with clear urethane. The window looks across red clay tiles, past *signor* Mario's woodlot and *signora* Francesca's rosemary bushes, beyond the red geraniums tumbling from the balcony of the last house on the street. We climb down the stairs to the front bedroom where my father will sleep and I open the balcony doors, which overlook the busy street below. The morning sun is high in the sky. Kathryn lies on my lap, I lie on Linda's and we sleep.

Shouts and rumbling noises wake us. Kathryn and Linda hurry to the balcony to see what's causing the commotion. A blue truck edges down our street. A man walking backwards directs the truck's progress with shouts and hand gestures: Joe. The driver has his head out the window, his dark hair brushing the front of the buildings. There are two passengers jammed in the front seat beside him: Bob and my father. Traffic backs up behind the truck and in front of it. Neighbours pour onto the street. The driver rolls up the tarpaulin that covers the back of the truck.

By the time we reach the street, a crowd has gathered. I don't know what the villagers do when we're not here, but when we are, it's as if they're on call. They're ready at a moment's notice, ready to help, to discuss, to organize, to suggest, to reorganize, to debate and finally, to cele-brate. The neighbours argue about who will unload the contents and where they will put them. First: six wooden ladder-backed chairs, with woven wicker seats. The old ladies examine every one for scratches or rough spots before the men are allowed to take them into the house. Second: a table with fat wooden legs, carved *a mano*, and a heavy marble top, streaked with charcoal and slate. Third: four fold-up beds, wrapped in heavy plastic. Fourth: a brown leather chesterfield. Fifth: a cardboard box.

"I'm not sure if it's a small refrigerator or a large toaster oven," says Bob, pointing to the box.

"Why didn't you ask Dad?"

"I did, but he answered me in Italian."

Angela comes out of her house, wiping her hands on her apron, smelling of rosemary and plum tomatoes.

"The paint," begins Angela, "is light and dark. *Perfetto*. Benito thought it's crazy to put in a brick fireplace, but it looks good. Everybody likes the bathroom the best. *Magnifico*, Joe."

"Angela, I was wondering, should we invite the neighbours in?"

"What for? The neighbours see your house every day. We all go in. Take a look. Everything — she looks good, no?"

As we walk down the street people call out from their open windows, "*Mezzabotte*, you are returned. *Benvenuto*." By the time, we've reached the corner, a three-minute walk, half an hour has passed. We stop at the bar to talk to Rocco and Joe and have a coffee. At the butcher shop, my father steps around the side of the building and knocks on the door. A woman comes out with a key and bends down and opens the lock on a garage door. Inside it's stacked to the ceiling with boxes of sheets, towers of fluffy comforters, piles of bath towels, and, since it's August, dangling from the ceiling are an assortment of inflatable water toys for the beach. My father does all the talking, arranges to buy the pillows and gives our address.

The pillows make it back to the house before we do. Angela has already stuffed them into pillowcases and arranged them on the beds. The merry clinking of goat bells comes jingling through the pasture near the church of San Nicola. Down our street walks a man with a bundle of sticks balanced on his head, a water jug in both hands.

"I put your supper on the kitchen table," says Angela. "Then, everyone goes straight to bed. That's enough for one day."

We awake the next morning to the sound of my father's shuffling feet and his face peering around our bedroom door. His expression is hesitant and apologetic; he is worried. His shirt is buttoned incorrectly and his shirttails hang unevenly.

"Let me fix it for you." I reach out my hand to the top buttonhole. In the middle of his chest is a large, yellow-green bruise and a crescent-shaped scar the shape of my mother's fingernail.

I can't breathe. I swallow hard, keep my voice calm.

"What's this all about, Dad?" I ask, nodding at the bruise, and resting my hand on his shoulder.

"You know your mother. She likes to jab sometimes. When she's yelling."

I want to button up the shirt and pretend I never saw the bruise. I want to phone my mother and demand an explanation. I want to find a way to keep my father in Supino. I want my father to be safe. But all I can do is rebutton his shirt, reassure him and watch as he and Bob head off to the bar for their coffee, together.

I wait for them in the shade of a nearby building beside a brown *cantina* door. Suddenly, the door opens. A wooden crate appears, along with a tiny woman dressed in a navy blue polka-dot dress. Her slender body is wrapped in a spotless cotton apron. Stepping into the street, she sets down the wooden crate, balancing it carefully on the wobbly cobblestones, swings a plastic bag of green spiky vegetables on top and says, *"Bella, no?"* Before I can answer, she disappears into the *cantina* and reappears a few seconds later with an eggplant in her hand. She crowns the pile of artichokes with the majestic purple vegetable, then looks up the street and sees my father. The colour drains from her face. She clutches her heart, tries to steady herself by grabbing the vegetable display.

"Fantasma. Spectro," she gasps, as the eggplant rolls from its throne and the artichokes go tumbling, spiky head over rounded tail, down the cobblestone street and into the gutter where they pick up speed before coming to rest on a grate.

My father approaches and talks to the woman like an old friend. She moves her hand away from her heart, touches his arm, cautiously, slowly. Then she laughs. They walk down the hill to pick up the spilled vegetables. The woman carries the artichokes back in her apron; my father holds the bruised eggplant in the crook of his arm. From inside the woman's *cantina* floats a lovely aroma: the fragrance of ripe peaches. I peek into the doorway as they return so that she invites me in saying, "*Vieni. Vieni.*" Inside the *cantina* are crates of vegetables and fruits arranged in a circle. Under the window, a brass scale catches the morning sunlight. A Havana cigar box, lire notes protruding from the partially opened lid, rests on a wooden shelf.

"What does *spectro* mean?"

"Ghost. Elena thought she saw the ghost of my brother, Americo, walking up the street. That scared her. Americo died 20 years ago."

My father, his hand in his back pocket, whistles softly, looking at the pile of watermelons. "Nice looking watermelons," he comments. I buy one and Bob carries it home.

"*Al fresco?*" asks our waiter. He seats us at a table, draped in white linen and set with cotton napkins and heavy silverware, in the yard beneath a kiwi tree. Rocco recommended this restaurant; they serve only pizza or antipasto on Saturday nights. The waiter, also known as Luigi the policeman or Domenico's son, stands notepad and pen in hand, waiting.

"What would you like to eat? They have pizza or antipasto," I tell my father.

"Whatever your mother says. Anything will do. Anything's fine."

"You can order whatever you want." But he can't. He

cannot choose. Trying to encourage my father to state his preference, to take what little power is granted, makes him uncomfortable. At home he eats what my mother cooks; he eats alone, sitting at the end of the kitchen table. He has no choice. Simple things, little things, are slowly taken away from him, a drop of water hitting the stone. Day after day. Year after year. Eventually hollowing the rock, making a hole.

The waiter brings four jugs of wine after we have ordered. "Didn't you tell him four *glasses* of wine?" I ask.

"So we take the rest home," he says. "Enjoy your dinner." In the darkness of evening my father begins to speak and his voice is different, younger, as if the *antipasto della montagna*, appetizers of the mountain, rejuvenate him. He talks about falling asleep in his olive tree on summer nights, listening to crickets and watching the brightest star over the church of San Cataldo. And he speaks about his mother, Filomena Corsi.

"A long time ago an army comes to Italy. They're going to Rome to fight, but they stop at Supino. Kill some men, rape the women. They take all the food and the horses they can find. Then, the army men leave. Go to Rome to fight. This army, they come from a place called Corsica. It's an island. Nine months pass. A lot of babies are born in Supino. Babies from these men who came to fight, you understand? No one knows what to do. They can't give the babies the name of the family. No one knows the name of the strangers — the barbarians. The people in the village go to the church and ask the priest what to do. The priest says, 'We give the babies a new name, a name of their own.'

And he baptizes all the babies *Corsi*, named for the place
Corsica, where the fathers come from. Your grandmother
she comes from that name. Filomena Corsi."

From the parking lot below, comes familiar sounds.
Car doors slam. Voices shout out greetings, as more and
more people arrive. Accompanying the footsteps and
laughter, a metallic jangle. Gypsies in brightly-coloured
clothes and jangling gold jewellry come walking over the
crest of the hill. The waiter quickly assesses the situation.
He claps his hands above his head and several men hurry
out carrying tables over their heads, starched white tablecloths over their arms. Soon the yard is full of tables,
chairs and laughter. The waiter goes from table to table
lighting the candles with his cigarette lighter. We're
surrounded by women, their hair slicked back with
fragrant oil, their earlobes heavy with golden hoops. Men,
in dark fitted pants and silk shirts, flash quick smiles.
Some carry babies, brilliant flowers or birds stitched onto
their little black vests, slipping them carefully into wicker-
seated high chairs. Someone pushes an old lady in a
wheelchair past our table and over to the corner where the
band is setting up. Beads and glittery stones decorate the
wheels so that as it bounces across the gravel sparks fly
like fireworks into the black night. A little girl, with curls
the colour of coal, skips around the tables, passing through
the squares of light cast by the restaurant windows. There's
a blur of streaming ribbons: red, yellow, blue and a flash of
golden bangles — and then she's gone — only to reappear
a moment later, her red clothes becoming flames in the
darkness. A five-piece band sets up in the corner. Before the

drummer has time to assemble his kit, they're playing *"La Bamba"*. The gypsies begin to dance and twirl among the tables set out beneath the disbelieving stars.

Before I know what's happening there's a noise behind me, the soft sound of footfall on gravel and a man beside the table holding out his hand who says, *"Vuoi ballare?"*

We dance among dark shadows, join hands and match our steps to theirs. There is laughter at every table, hands clapping, feet anxious to spin and whirl upon the gravel dance floor. When we leave the restaurant that evening, we float down the hill to the sound of guitar strings. By the time we reach the archway of slender beechnut trees, the air is silent.

Angela stands in the doorway of our house. She has a small bowl of eggs in one hand and a basket of plum tomatoes in the other. Out of the pocket of her apron hangs a bouquet of fresh basil, tied with twine. We take these gifts to Sunday lunch at Guido's, passing a dozen villagers as we walk down the hill calling, *"Buon giorno, buon giorno"* to people pushing strollers, walking arm in arm, carrying gifts. We pass the Bar Italia, where the flower shop man is playing cards with Bruno, so my father waves his bouquet of basil leaves, a bandleader waving his baton as we all march down the street.

The pastry shop is crowded with people standing in the doorway, talking, joking amid the warm sugary aroma of fresh baking. As the church bell begins to swing, the villagers look at their watches. Parcels of pastries, with golden curls of ribbon hanging down the sides, appear overhead, passed from hand to hand, from the front counter to the doorway of the shop. Folded lire are passed in the other direction. Then, as the bells subside, the bakery crowd disperses and the street is deserted, except for the baker calling from behind the counter, "*Buon pranzo. Buon pranzo.*"

Guido looks up from the table outside his house, where he's grating a piece of parmesan cheese. He covers the plate with a tea towel and comes to undo the latch on the gate. He shakes hands with my father, kisses him and says, "*Buon giorno, zio.* Would you like to see the garden?"

Luigina is in the garden. She wipes her hands on her apron before she greets us and acknowledges my father first, although she's never met him. She keeps her arm on his shoulder as Guido hustles a brown leather armchair and sets it near the corner of the house. Luigina dusts the polished seat with the corner of her apron before saying, "Sit. Sit. Lunch is almost ready."

At the side of the house, beneath a long arbour of grapevines, several tables are pushed together. They're covered with tablecloths: linen, gingham, one faded pink damask. In the centre of each table is a row of crusty Italian bread rolls. The tables are set with mismatched plates and glasses and large cotton napkins. I do a quick count: 17 places.

"*Tutta la famiglia?*" asks my father.

"*Sí. Certo,*" responds Guido. "They all come."

Guido's four sons and their families live in Rome, Frosinone and Morolo, but every Sunday they come home to Supino for lunch. They take the train to the Ferentino station, the bus to the Kennedy Bar and then they walk up the hill to this little three-room house. By one o'clock, there's a bouquet of red roses on one table, a box of chocolates on another and two trays of pastries on the kitchen windowsill, waiting. Our bouquet is hanging upside down on the side of the kitchen cupboard. Guido opens two gallons of home-made wine, one red and one white. Soon the air is full of voices. By the time the empty trays of antipasto leave the table and the fresh egg noodles arrive, my father is animated, in the arms of his family.

When my father came to Canada, he left behind a girl-friend. She lived at the end of his street. He didn't tell me her name, only that she had "*capelli d'oro*," golden curls like my daughter Kathryn's, and brown eyes, "shiny as chestnuts." He said, "If she sees me walking down the path, even after all these years, she'll run and throw her arms around me. She'll be that happy to see me."

When we had said goodbye to my mother in Toronto she had said, "Take him and don't bring him back. You're wasting your money. Everyone he knew is dead. You'll see. You'll be sorry." My mother stood in the doorway, arms crossed, her face wrinkled in a permanent frown. My father shrugged his shoulders, tried to speak, choked a little on the words. If he'd stayed in Supino, married the girl near his house, would he be like Guido, have a family like this one?

With the appearance of another platter of food and the smell of the roasted chicken and rosemary and the scent of the lemons all the way from Sorrento and the sound of the knife slicing through coarse Italian bread, my father tells a story.

"Guido. Do you remember *pazzo* Lorenzo?" Crazy Larry was the town hermit, walked with a limp and lived in the woods behind my father's farm. "He only came into the village to steal things — chickens, grapes. Once he took a ricotta right out of my mother's pan. Wouldn't listen to anyone, except my father. Of course, my father shot him in the leg. Just that one time. Didn't kill him. Just slowed him down a little."

After lunch a woman joins us. White curls bounce beneath a black beret and her eyes are very bright. My father runs to meet her and for a long time after they sit together in the corner, not talking much, but leaning; her head toward his, as if she doesn't want to miss a word. No wedding band. Just a silver locket around her neck.

The next morning as we walk down Via D'Italia to the Bar Italia, we get almost to the house where the parrot calls out "*Ciao*," when Rocco salutes, "*Mezzabotte*. How are you?" Bob and I go into the bar, order our cappuccini and bring my father's outside to him. All the tables and chairs are still stacked inside the bar. Rocco pushes through the crowd, a chair held high in the air. He sets the chair in the centre of the patio in the heart of a gathering crowd.

Rocco emerges from the crowd, leans his foot against the wall and begins, "Some fool at City Hall went to Toronto for a conference. He came back with a Canadian idea. Apparently, in Toronto, there is a fee for using patio space. The cafe owner has to pay for the use of the outdoor area, correct?" Bob nods yes; Rocco shakes his head. "So," he continues, "the fool brings the idea to Supino. The Council agree to try it. They passed a motion that bar owners must pay a fee to use the patio space. Why would you pay a fee to sit outside?"

Supino's all-purpose blue truck, with the official emblem painted in gold on the side, drives quickly up the street and turns wildly onto the side street behind the Bar Italia. The passenger, in dark glasses with his cap pulled low over his head, tosses a paper out the window and the car speeds up the street and out of sight.

"*Vigliaccheria!*" calls someone from the crowd. "Coward," translates Rocco as he grabs the paper, glances at it quickly and calls for Bruno.

The fine. Already I hear them arguing about the young police officer, his father would have ripped the fine into shreds and thrown it on the floor of the *municipio*. Someone calls out to the green grocer next door and he laughs and tosses a lemon into the crowd. In a moment, the paper's back in Rocco's hand, only now it's tied around a lemon, held on with a couple of elastic bands. The blue truck comes barrelling down the street again and as it curves around the telephone booth, Rocco tosses the lemon into the sunroof. The crowd laughs.

"I think by Thursday, Friday at the latest, they repeal the law."

The crowd begins to scatter, the villagers going about their daily chores.

Before we go Rocco tells us that the scaffolding across

the street came from another American idea. "Joe from Quattro Strade emigrated to Detroit. 1954. Last year, he comes back. He bought a little farm down there, grows some good grapes. He had this idea to give a gift to the town, so he put some money up to make a house for pensioners, a retirement home. It's an American idea to put old people in a special house, no? By the time they put up the scaffolding, they ran out of money. It's crazy anyway. No one in Supino would put their parents in a home. Their parents have their own houses."

The day before we went to the cemetery, I checked with Rocco, who, as usual, assured me, "No problem, Maria. There's a man there every morning, except Sunday, between 10:00 a.m. and 1:00 p.m. — maybe, 12:30 p.m. if it's a hot day. His name is Maurizio. He's been there a long time, since 1940, or maybe '41. Anyway, Maurizio's got all the records. He knows everything. Write down the name of your grandparents, the date of death and show him the paper. He'll take you right to the grave."

We drive through the laneway of trees that marks the end of Supino Centro and stop for directions at the first house we see. An elderly man sits in his wheelchair on the cement verandah of a fairly modern-looking home. He's digging in a planter box. At the top of the stairway lies a thick tree branch on an angle, to keep the wheelchair and the man from rolling down the stairs.

"*Buon giorno*," Bob calls from the car window and the old man cups his hand around his ear. A younger man, dressed in blue jeans and a John Lennon T-shirt, jumps on his motor scooter and roars the few metres down his driveway to our car.

"*Americana*?" he asked, addressing Kathryn, who is sitting in the back seat, while peering at her over his sunglass frames.

"*Canadese*," she says. "Do you speak English?"

"I get by with a little help from my friends."

"Can you give us directions to the cemetery?"

"*Il cimitero*? The long and winding road," he begins. Then he revs the engine of his motor scooter and motions us to follow him. Before we have a chance to respond, he's pulled in front of our car and is roaring down the street. When we reach the cemetery our guide pulls up beside the window of the back seat and the young man turns to my father and speaks for a few minutes in Italian. He flashes a big smile, looks again at Kathryn and calls out, "*Ciao bella*," before he roars off.

"What's that all about?" Bob asks.

"There's a concert tonight at San Sebastiano," explains my father. "The boy wants Kathryn to go."

"What did you say?" ask Bob and Kathryn in unison.

"Sure, might as well. Everybody goes. We all go."

At the cemetery entrance is a small office. Empty. The gate is open. Wildflowers grow among its iron bars and a vine, with pale moonflowers, has wrapped itself around the supporting post. We start down one path, reading the gravestones as we stroll along.

"Here's one," calls Kathryn.

It's a marble stone with "Coletta" carved deeply across

the top. It's too new to be my grandparents, but it is the marker of my uncle Enrico Coletta. There's even a photo of *zio* Enrico attached to the stone within some kind of plastic bubble. The stone has the date of birth carved on it, 1890, but no date of death.

"Kathryn, when your great-grandmother was expecting her second baby, her husband went to America for two years to work. When he came back, Americo was already walking. He started to cry when he saw my father. He didn't know who he was. My father got to calling him Americo, because he was born when Papa was in America. I never knew his name was Enrico until I saw his passport. Everybody in the village called him Americo, from the money he earned in America."

"Is that how your father bought the farm, from the money he earned in America?"

"No, he bought it later, after I had come to Canada. Regina and I sent money home. When he died he left the farm to me. I own it."

Suddenly my father looks pale. His breathing, usually so slow and even, is hurried. I can hear him gasping in the hot, still air. His body sways a little in the heat as he rubs his hand over his eyes. I put out my hand to steady him. We walk over to a bench near some evergreen trees and sit down.

"It's not so good to see your name on a grave," he declares. We sit in the silence of the cemetery, waiting and looking at each other. He runs his hand over his face, digs in his pocket for his handkerchief, blows his nose, but his eyes are rimmed with red when he looks at me.

My father explains that he was thinking about Philip, my nephew, my brother Don's youngest son. Philip had been killed three years ago in a welding accident at his job site. He was 23.

I remember the smells of the funeral parlour, the stunned and sunburned faces of dozens of young people. There were white flowers everywhere.

"That day your mother told me to get in the car and we drove up the highway. I must have fallen asleep, but all of a sudden I was standing in front of a tombstone. It said Coletta. I thought it was my tombstone," he explains. "I thought I was dead. It should have been me," he adds quietly, leaning forward, with his hands on his knees. "Philip should be here. I should be dead."

We never found my grandparents' graves. We came across a section of stones, flat and worn near the juniper trees, moss growing on many of them, but names and dates had been worn away. Perhaps these were their markers; maybe I only needed to believe that they were.

It's almost eight o'clock and I am just closing the front door behind me as I leave when Angela calls across the street, "You'll need a sweater. It's cold when the sun goes down." We file down the street and by the time we've reached the corner, grandmothers, children, young teens, dogs, everyone of every age is walking leisurely down the hill. At the Bar Italia, some of the crowd veer off to have a beer and a chat with friends who have walked down from Via Piagge or one of the other streets on the eastern side of town. The rest of us continue through the narrowest part of the street where all the shopkeepers are closing their doors, drawing heavy accordion grates across their display windows.

We stop for a few minutes at the flower shop to help Fiore, the owner, carry several tropical plants across the street. He likes these plants to get the early morning sun, so he's chiselled several ledges out of the stone opposite his store. Fiore nestles the clay pots in for the evening. In the early morning, their leaves will be misty with dew. By the time he has opened his shop for business the sunlight will have evaporated the dewdrops and left the leaves vibrant.

The woman at the butcher's shop tosses a bone to each of the dogs lined up in front of the store. We pass her and approach the crossroads at the side of the church of Santa Maria Maggiore. People from this vantage point can see other villagers as they come out of the church or the shops, or up from the small tunnel that runs between the jewellry store and the dry cleaners. There is always a chorus of greetings, accentuated by car horns and church bells. Tonight those sounds are joined by the murmurs from inside the church, the heavy doors propped open in the evening heat, as the parishioners recite the prayers of the rosary.

"There's a feast here in June, or maybe July, after the cherries have finished, but before the tomatoes and peppers turn red. Everyone who lives in Supino draws patterns on the pavement. Then they fill in the design with flower petals from the wildflowers on the mountain.

There's a mass at San Cataldo and then the priest and the altar boys walk down the hill to this church and up the hill to San Nicola. My mother used to make special cookies for this *festa*. If there are fireworks left over from the feast of San Cataldo, they shoot them off. Mama never let Regina and I stay in town for the fireworks. She said it was too late. We had to sneak out the window and climb up onto the roof to see them."

Down at the end of the roadway, the tables and chairs from the Kennedy Bar take over most of the street. Along the sidewalk, swerving between couples and strollers and tooting his horn, comes the young man who gave us the directions to the cemetery this morning. Carlo. He parks his motor scooter and reaches out his hand to my father. "*Buona sera, signor,*" he says as he motions us across the street to join the group of villagers heading toward a set of stairs cut out of a steep hill. We climb the stairs with everyone else, strollers lifted between couples, young people with their arms tucked into the arm of their grandparent, kids who run up four or five stairs, then down two, then up again. At the top of the stairs, rows of white plastic patio chairs are set up on the grass with extra seating around the perimeter in the form of planks and overturned plastic pop crates. At the far end a stage made of scaffolding boards is propped on a foundation of cement blocks. In the corner are two metal playground slides with a rope stretched between them and bedspreads clothes-pegged around their frame to create a sort of impromptu dressing room. On the other side of the stage is an engraved wooden lectern.

"*Gelato?*" asks the young man before he dashes off, returning with his hands full of lemons and his pockets full of plastic spoons. The lemons have been hollowed out and filled with lemon sherbet. Children chase each other in the dark, racing in and out of the rows of chairs, and old men lean on their canes, talking. From somewhere near the back of the crowd, a cheer erupts and applause flutters into the night. Rocco moves to the lectern and says a few quick sentences in Italian and raises his hand as if the concert will begin, but then glances toward us and says, "*Scusa. Le Canadese.* Sorry, allow me to translate for you, our Canadian visitors. We have a folkloric group from Veroli, a small town just past Frosinone; we have a band of musicians from Morolo; and we have a film for children, '*Topo Gigio.*'" From behind the bedspreads comes a lively little band, led by a man playing the *organetto*. The band, outfitted in white shirts with red vests, moves through the crowd working its way to the stage, the villagers clapping along with the music. At intermission Bob and Carlo order pizza — *margherita, napoli, bianca* — while my father, Kathryn, and I sit on the marble step of the jewellry store. After the intermission, the children's film is shown on the makeshift bedspread screen and though there's a soundtrack, the children are so involved in sharing the storyline with each other and yelling out advice and encouragement for the cartoon characters that it's very difficult to actually hear it. Some of the babies and toddlers in the crowd have fallen asleep on the shoulders of adults or curled up on makeshift beds made from facing chairs.

After the film, folkloric dancers come whirling out from behind the bedspread onto the stage. The children jump from their seats, some reenacting the scenes from "*Topo Gigio*", others dancing in the aisles. On the stage, the dancers make a circle and a young couple step into the centre, placing their hands on each other's shoulders. The audience claps encouragingly, as the couple spin around faster and faster and the dancers that encircle them sway from side to side, the women with their skirts held in their hands and the men with their hands clasped behind their backs, occasionally calling out, "*Ey!*" as they stomp their feet. The original couple, now spinning in a whirlpool of red skirt and green vest and white cotton, are joined by a second couple and in a few more minutes a third couple. Pools of light interrupt the darkness, the twirling dancers wind into view and then go spinning off into the shadows.

When the dance concludes the villagers gather up sweaters, their sleeping children and head off into the night. Within minutes, the crowd has left the hilltop.

Rocco joins us as we are preparing to leave and says, "In Supino we have to make our own small entertainment, otherwise our young people will leave the village to go to Rome or Frosinone. Every year the Council supports the *Este Di Supino*. Summer in Supino. Every evening, except Sunday, we have something — tomorrow is a movie, "*Mediterraneo*." The next night is a magician and the Supino marching band. On Friday it is amateur band night and Carlo has a band that will perform."

We leave Rocco and Carlo at the bottom of the stairs,

with a promise to return to the park on Friday. As we climb the hill, the noises of the street diminish and the night grows dark and silent.

In the morning, when Kathryn opens the shutters of the front bedroom, people are already on the street, their baskets hooked over their arms. We join the parade of villagers walking briskly down the hill and as soon as we've turned from Via Condotto Vecchio onto Via D'Italia we see the multicoloured awnings of the market stalls. A few fruit and vegetable vendors have parked three-wheel pickup trucks and sit behind piles of crates. You can smell the peaches before you see them — *"Fresca, fresca."* At the end of the street are three barrels of watermelons. A hose stretches from a nearby garage to keep the melons cold in the August heat. We walk the length of the street, admiring the produce. We would like to buy something, but we know if we do, Joe will say, "Why you buy this? I got peaches in my yard. What's the matter with you, Bob? You don't like my peaches?" and if we buy eggplants or onions for Angela, she'll accept them, with a shake of her head, and then have us over for lunch to eat them. We do buy six lemons the size of grapefruits, which my father claims are so sweet you can make a salad with them and not put in any sugar.

"It's your uncle Fidel's 50th anniversary party next month. Maybe a gift from Supino, to make it special. What do you think?"

The woman in the stall pulls out a handmade lace

cloth from one of the boxes stacked beneath the table. The cloth is crocheted with a very fine cotton thread. There's a row of hemstitching at both ends. I leave them to haggle over the price and count out the lire. We meet them back at the Bar Italia, but it's too hot and the bartender's too busy to make cappuccini so we have *aranciata* instead.

"I bought a basket," I announce, holding up the wicker purchase.

"My father used to make baskets like this," my father says. "Mostly for my mother and my aunts, but sometimes to sell at the market. I learned it when I was a boy. On Palm Sunday, we'll get the palm after mass and I'll fold it a few times and make a cross for you. That's how my father taught me. But you have to wait for the spring. That's when the vines and the willow branches are easy to bend. We went into the vineyard or the woods to get the skinny branches. The vines like to dry slowly, take their time to learn the shape of the basket."

On the way home we pass the watermelon vendor and the usual group of young boys, about eight or ten years old, with their soccer ball. As soon as the watermelon man moves on, they can reclaim that end of the street for their usual pre-lunch soccer game. My father hands the man a lira note, calls out to the boys, tossing the watermelon toward the cement step. The melon shatters into jagged red chunks and the boys grab pieces and stuff them into their mouths.

"*Grazie, Mezzabotte,*" they shout.

❖

Today my father approaches his farm, one hand in his back pocket, the other unhooking the tattered twine that holds the gate in place. Sixty-four years ago he hooked the rope over the fence post, straightened the collar of his new woollen jacket, patted the leather passport and headed down the hill to the train station for Rome and Genoa and then for Canada by ship. His short fingers grasp the loop of twine, the scar on his left thumbnail where he hit it with an axe while chopping wood one winter white against his suntanned hands, rough with years of work. He lifts the gate slightly and it swings open, creaking rustily. The squeaking gate represents neglect. Sadness lives in the slump of his shoulders, in the stillness of his hands. He must have imagined, all these years, that these people were taking care of his home. Now he leans over the gate fingering the hinges powdered with rust. The neighbour stands behind him anxiously drumming his fingers against the leg of his work pants.

"We made a new gate to save walking out to the road and back in again. A big metal gate — the one you drove through on the way in. It opens automatically. You only have to push the button. You know how it is, *Mezzabotte, moderno, progresso, automatico.*"

My father walks the path of ancient grapevines, nodding his head in approval. The soil beneath them is freshly turned, the posts that support the branches are sturdy and straight. He stops to caress a dusty leaf that shades a heavy bunch of burgundy grapes. He rests his hand on the trunk of the cherry tree and tries to slide his fingers between the smooth bark and the rocky wall of the house. Behind the farmhouse, the vegetable patch is full of tomato, pepper and zucchini plants. The zucchini vines have travelled over the fence, tumbling into the larger yard next door. The garden ends where the rocky soil of the mountain begins. He throws some grain to the four plump chickens calling from the coop, picks up a couple of pieces of kindling that have slipped from the woodpile and replaces them carefully. He pats a metal pan with holes in the bottom hanging on the wall.

"Your grandmother made cheese," he tells me. "Balls of fresh mozzarella. Sometimes ricotta — small circles, like a pie, with curved edges. She made lunch for the priest every day. He lived beside the church — Santa Maria — and after mass I waited to ask him what he would like to eat. One day he said, *'Pollo,'* but I reminded him, 'It's Friday. No meat today, Father.' And you know what he told me? He said, *'Pollo* is poultry, *carne* is meat.' I had to eat bread and cheese — same as every Friday. My mother said the priest says what he eats in his house, but she says what we eat in ours."

My grandmother had not followed the tradition of the village; she had not given one of her sons to the church. The first son, Giacomo, she gave to her country. He joined King Umberto's army, fought in the war. Giacomo was gone for seven years and when he returned he was a changed man. She never asked him about those years. Instead, twice a week, she made his favourite meal: ricotta-filled ravioli.

Her second son belonged to the land. It was his place

to work beside his father and learn the ways of the earth, the cycles of the seasons. Americo was patient with the tedious tasks of the farmyard: splitting firewood, picking olives, trimming artichokes. In November she knit him a woollen cap and because he didn't like the brightness of the white wool, she dyed it by soaking it in a pail of rainwater and licorice sticks.

Then came the twin boys, Pietro and Nicolo. My grandfather, Domenico, pruned grapevines and wove them into a cradle. Two weeks in the sunshine and the cradle was as sturdy as hardwood. The aunts, who lived up on the mountain, lined the inside with sheep's wool. When Domenico covered them at night, the brothers always had a hand, or a foot, touching each other. It was the serious Pietro who walked first. He stood, his chubby legs spread far apart, at the doorway of the farmhouse waiting for Nicolo. That April morning, Nicolo lay listless in the cradle. Pietro sat on the floor, beside the cradle expecting Nicolo to reach out his hand, climb over the side of the cradle, and toddle to the door. But the influenza epidemic had come to Supino. Nicolo never woke from the fever.

Pietro lay beside the cradle holding the hand of his dead brother and no one had the heart to move him. At twilight, Domenico brought warm milk from the neighbour's cow for Pietro.

My grandmother said, "Look how he sleeps. Like an angel." But he was not sleeping. Pietro was dead. My grandfather lifted the empty cradle, took it outside. The night was dark. He dropped the cradle on the pathway. He smashed his foot down, again and again, snapping the vines. He struck a match against the cement and threw it at the pile of twigs.

The priest blessed the twin babies, and comforted my grandmother, but Domenico would not come into the house. He stood in the yard, stared at the ashes. The priest approached him slowly, not wishing to intrude on his sorrow. He could see that Domenico was consumed. They walked down the hill together to the tiny church of San Sebastiano and, in the back room, the priest assembled a table and two chairs. He brought two glasses and a bottle of whiskey. Domenico returned home the next day at noon. He never spoke of that night.

After my grandparents buried their two sons they had two daughters, Angelina and Regina. My grandmother's hair was white by the time my father was born. The seventh child is a lucky omen. By tradition this baby belonged to the church. She named the baby Loreto, an ancient name derived from the word *lauretum*, which means laurel grove. My grandmother believed the legend of Loreto, a northern town situated in a laurel grove atop a hill near the Adriatic Coast, not too far from Ancona. She knew that during the night of December 10th, over 600 years ago, a host of angels had placed the home of Mary, Joseph and Jesus in the hilltop town. The angels had flown the sacred home from its original setting in Palestine and then across the Adriatic Sea to Italy. The simple cottage rested there, among the laurel leaves, and over the years, princes and popes had arranged for a tremendous sanctuary to be built around the Holy House. My grandmother had heard stories of the construction that had lasted for more than 300 years. She'd heard about the famous painters and sculptors that had worked there. She'd heard that the base of marble that surrounded the little house had been worn down like a furrow in a field by the many pilgrims who had gone to kneel and pray before the Santa Casa. My grandmother did not need to see the sacred home of the Holy Family to know the legend was true. The day the priest came to see the infant he said, "Keep your baby, Filomena. You have given enough."

In the August daylight my father's farmhouse seems smaller than before. Sunshine pours through the open door into its emptiness. My father runs his finger along a post.

"Here it is," he announces. "On this nail, my mother kept a cross. *Nonno* carved it from an olive branch. It's a soft wood with a good smell. After *nonno* carved it, Mama hung it here over the bed. *Nonno* always sat in the corner and carved. In the dark, you never knew if he was there or not until you heard the sound of his knife shaving the wood. In the morning, my mother gathered those shavings to start the fire. After Giacomo married the girl from town, he and his bride came to this house. The girl said, 'Why do you leave the old man in the corner where it's dark?' She didn't know he was blind. My father gave them a little piece of land near the road. Giacomo built a house there."

Now only a corner is left, two crumbly walls smeared with patches of cement. Giacomo's original house would have been the size of my garden shed. His grandchildren expanded it to a three-story farmhouse.

"That's a tiny house."

"Well sure, but there were only two people. And Giacomo and his wife — they were pretty thin."

We pass the cherry tree and the three olive trees that are part of the original farm.

"Your aunt Regina and I used to sit on the roof and pluck the cherries from this tree. On the night of the feast of San Cataldo, there were fireworks. You could see them all over the village. When it got dark, your aunt would hang two cherry stems over her ears and she'd say, 'I am the queen of Supino. Let the fireworks begin.'"

The people who live on the other side of my father's land have a stucco house with an olive grove in the backyard and red roses in front. Sitting beneath the chestnut tree, we drink wine from last year's grape harvest.

"I had trouble finding this street today," Bob tells them. "After two years, we've already forgotten, but Maria's father remembered the way."

"It's a steep path. Hard to find," my father tells Bob. Then turning to me he says, "Even your grandfather lost his way home once. Papa had too much to drink one night at a cousin's wedding. Some of my uncles brought him home. Of course, they'd been drinking too, so they left him at the wrong house."

These neighbours call my father *Mezzabotte*, speak to him as if he never left the village.

Bob and my father walk down to the bar each morning for coffee and sit watching the children play, the housewives walking to town to do their shopping. When the sun rises past the bell tower and Bruno lowers the canvas awning over the patio, Bob orders a cappuccino to go and brings it up to the house for me. Bruno didn't have any cups for such a request, so the first morning Bob carried the cappuccino in a ceramic cup and saucer under a cloth napkin. All the old women sweeping their front steps stopped and chattered to each other, "What could it mean?" By the second day, Bruno has worked out a plan: he pours the cappuccino into a paper Pepsi cup. I don't know what causes more of a stir: coffee in a paper cup or the realization that this is a man who takes cappuccino to his wife *every* morning. While I sit on the balcony, Bob takes the broom from the closet to sweep the front steps. Half a dozen housewives come running. One woman grabs the broom from Bob's hand and refuses to return it. Angela hurries over to explain that Bob is using the wrong broom. That's an indoor broom with soft bristles for sweeping marble or ceramic tiles. For the cement steps you have to use an outdoor broom.

My father and I head down Via D'Italia on our way to the barber shop. Suddenly — out of nowhere — a basket drops in front of me. A rope's attached to the basket so I follow it up to the third-floor balcony. Hanging out of the window is an old man. The next thing I know, my father's on his way up the stairs to visit and I'm on my way to buy bread and coffee for the old man with the money he lowered in the basket.

At the *tabacchi* store, I point to the bread behind the counter and chop the back of one hand onto the palm of the other, asking the woman to slice it in half. There are about a dozen brands of coffee lined up on the shelf. I pantomime the circumstances and throw in some Italian phrases until the woman behind the counter nods and says, "*Alberto antico. Sí, sí.*" She picks a blue packaged brick of coffee from the wall behind her, puts it and the bread into a bag and tosses in a little strawberry-filled candy. When I get back, I put the plastic bag in the basket, ring the doorbell and he hauls up the basket as my father comes downstairs.

"When that man was a boy, his father gave him a calf to take care of, same as me. We walked up the mountain together some mornings. It took three hours. There's a beautiful stream near the top of the path, with cold water running from a spout stuck in the side of a rock. I used to stop there for a drink. I had three aunts who lived on the mountain, so everyday I had three breakfasts. At the top the cows would graze and we'd talk. I named my cow Giardinella, the gardener. She gave 10 quarts of milk a day. I walked to town, left a quart at the church and the rest at the houses in the village. After the feast of San Cataldo, Giardinella's calf was ready to be sold at the market in Frosinone, 30 miles away. On Saturday morning my father and I walked the calf there. It was a nice walk with the sun on our backs and some bread and cheese in our pockets. It was a hard walk back though, if we didn't sell the calf. The calf couldn't walk both ways. If we didn't sell her, we had to carry her back."

When my father's family bought Giardinella it marked the end of his formal education, grade three. Alberto was in the same situation. They were sorry to leave school; there was more they wanted to learn. Alberto liked to read. My father learned numbers, added them in his head without a pencil.

"I couldn't read well until I came to Canada. I learned English by reading the newspaper. Your aunt Regina used to buy it for me," my father said.

Today, we walk single-file in the shade of the buildings, but the stone walls hold no coolness from the previous night. We're on our way to the Kennedy Bar to buy a bottle of *Mille Fiori* to take to Angela's house for lunch. My father is showing us a "shortcut." He climbs a set of narrow, crumbling cement steps. If I'd noticed them before I thought they belonged to someone's house, or garden, but they lead to a narrow pathway and more steps. We climb and climb like a small herd of mountain goats, heads down, concentrating on the rocky terrain, trusting his memory. In a few minutes we reach an abandoned house. A huge rock face separates it from another house, three stories high. Someone has chiselled ledges from the stone, five narrow tiers, and in every space, containers the size of a tomato paste tin to a 10-quart plaster pail are crammed with blooming geraniums. Geraniums hang from baskets too, dozens of delicate petals of blazing colour — white, red, and pink — like the embers of a campfire when the wind blows up from the lake.

A woman opens the door of the house and carefully steps outside, bringing a bucket of water and a long-handled ladle. She's a little woman, dressed in black, with a white apron and white hair pulled back in a braid and twisted round her head. She speaks with my father for a moment or two, then offers us water from her bucket. The water's cool, refreshing. As she climbs the rocks to water her flower garden we continue on our way.

The passageway widens to accommodate a donkey carrying a bag of cement. It carries bags of cement from the *piazza* in front of San Nicola, where the road narrows and the cobblestone steps begin, to the stone house someone from Rome is renovating as a weekend home. My father knew its original owners, went to school with the son and daughter in the family though they were a few years older. Their father used this place to sleep when he collected the olives, but the rest of the family had lived with their grandfather in town. The foundation and one wall of the house remain from the 40s when it was bombed during the war. The older villagers are worried its history is bad luck and feel it is too high on the mountainside to be safe.

Now, rock music blares from an upstairs window. A motor scooter leans against a doorway. A man comes out of the darkness of a *cantina* wearing a blood-stained apron and carrying a large knife. Behind him a ceramic bowl full of meat chunks and branches of rosemary sit on a table ready to be made into sausages. A leg of pork, or maybe lamb, hangs in the corner on a silver meat hook. Raising the knife, he shouts at us, "Bob! Remember me? I'm

Rocco's uncle. I meet you in Toronto, last year."

Bob shakes hands with the man and comments on the heat.

"Thirty-four degrees," replies Rocco's uncle. "What we need is some peaches and white wine. *Fresca*. Come in. Come in."

My father is already inside the house. The Supinese cannot imagine an encounter that doesn't call for wine, a little fruit, some cookies.... In the kitchen, the air is cool and a woman, I assume she is Rocco's aunt, whisks the flowers off the table, replacing them with a bowl of peaches and three sweating green wine bottles. Without a word Rocco's aunt collects an assortment of plates, fruit knives and clear glasses from her cupboards and distributes them.

"The peach," begins Rocco's uncle, caressing its skin, "is silken in texture, immensely fragrant. Slice the peach," he says as he slices the fruit and stuffs the pieces into a glass. "Then, pour a little wine on the top," he continues, filling the glass to the brim. He stabs the knife into one of the peaches waiting in the bowl and hands it to my father.

"My grandfather used to eat his peaches like this," my father says. "*Nonno* was blind, but when he cut those peaches, perfect slices, every one exactly the same. Sometimes he poured red wine instead of white. Your aunt Angelina — she brought the wrong bottle. But your grandfather, he didn't like red wine so much. He'd start to yell. She liked to tease the blind *nonno*. She brings red wine on purpose, then she runs away."

Peaches and white wine: deceptively simple and quietly potent. After three or four glasses, my memory is as fuzzy as the fruit. Then Rocco's aunt speaks, pointing her finger at each of us in turn, counting our heads as she circles the room, *"Uno, due...sette."* She cracks one egg for each person into a bowl. One of the eggs has a little piece of straw still stuck to its side. Swirling the eggs with a wooden spoon she adds handfuls of flour until she has a soft ball of dough. She pulls the gingham cloth from the tabletop with one hand and dumps the dough onto the table with the other, reaches behind the kitchen door for the rolling pin. She stretches that ball of dough into a creamy yellow circle and sprinkles the dough with flour. Before the dust can settle she flips the circle, over and over, into a long roll. Using a sharp steel knife, she slices through the roll at exact intervals, lifting each section, opening out the noodles as if she is displaying an assortment of satin ribbons. With a slight rotation of her wrist, she places the noodles back on the table, nests of egg fettuccine.

"Aspetta. Cinque minuti," she says. "Wait. Five minutes."

As children we sat and ate these same noodles in Aunt Regina's dining room, on Geoffrey Street, with the black-and-white photos of the Supino relatives hanging on the walls. They watched us eat.

"Pesto is the poetry of the fields," informs Rocco's uncle. "For a classic poem, you must pick the best words, arrange them perfectly. The same with pesto. Instead of words, we use ingredients from the fields: basil, garlic, olive oil. They must be of the finest quality to create the finest poetry. You understand? Look at this basil plant. It grows in the window facing the Mediterranean Sea. The wind carries its salty breezes across the mountains to this house. My wife tells me her cousin in Detroit makes pesto in a blender. *Automatico*. Absolutely unacceptable. You must use a marble mortar to release the fragrance. The pesto requires circular motion....

A fragrance fills the room. I lose myself in the scent, the aroma, too *squisito* to describe. There are ancient trees in Supino, with bark as black and wrinkled as a burnt log, with leaves, grey and slender, like a weeping willow. The olives have been plucked from these trees, the oil gently extracted from the first press. And the wine. Not the clear, light white wine we've been drinking all morning, but red wine: woody, rich, full bodied. It slides down my throat with the coolness of November twilight on the mountain, and the warmth of the noon Supino sun. Five minutes later, we're ready to eat.

En route to the Kennedy Bar, still in search of *Mille Fiori*, we pause beside a three-story yellow stucco building outlined with golden trim. It has new windows with aluminum frames and flower boxes made of wrought iron. It's the only building I've seen in Supino that has an indoor courtyard. Across the arched doorway there's an ornate iron fence painted coal black with a locked gate. Beyond that gate is a cobblestone square with large potted palm trees and a curved marble stairway climbing to upper floors. Bar Centrale is on the first floor. Despite this, my father informs me this is the priest's house.

"The priest's family lived in Rome, but they owned a few buildings in Supino. They came in the summer time, when it's too hot in Rome. Like a cottage. His brother had the bar. No, maybe it was a cousin. I don't remember. The priest didn't own it," he assures me. "He just had a drink there, in the evening, you know, after mass."

There's a war monument in the *piazza* outside the bar, a young soldier, standing proud with the Italian flag clutched in his hand. At the base of the statue, etched into the marble, are the names of the soldiers from Supino. There's one section for the First World War and three sections for the Second World War. Giacomo was my father's oldest brother, a gentle man who would have preferred to stay on the farm with his family, his grapes and his dog Nero, but the war came and Giacomo left. My father was only nine when Giacomo went to fight. One day, months after Giacomo had left, my father and his friend Antonio were playing war and fashioning guns with some branches they'd cut, when his mother came rushing out of the house. She grabbed the stick from my father's hand, and broke it over her knee. "You think war is a game?" she asked, but before he could say a word, she'd gone back in the house, crying. My father said it was the only time she'd ever raised her voice at him, the only time he'd ever seen her truly angry. Giacomo couldn't write, but it didn't matter anyway. His mama couldn't read. All she could do was wait.

Every day, inside the house, his mother waited while Nero waited outside by the gate. By the time the war was over, they had eaten all but three of their chickens and Nero had grey hairs in his black coat, his face thin and drawn. Then, one evening, when the family was inside eating supper, a strange dog barked. My grandfather went for his gun. There'd been a lot of rabid foxes in the area and he didn't trust strays. It was Nero barking. Suddenly, a tall, slim figure appeared at the gate, bending to pat the dog. My grandfather called out to the stranger to be careful, the dog was rabid, but the man called back, "*É Giacomo, Papa.*" My grandmother flew from the house, down the grapevine path and into the arms of her son. They roasted a chicken that night and Nero never barked again.

There's a small grocery store tucked in behind the Bar Centrale and from the upstairs window comes the sound of someone's radio. In the thin strip of shade produced by the laundry baking on the clothesline lies a mangy old dog, panting in the afternoon heat. At the top of the hill is a broken cement square, with chicory plants poking through its cracks, their purple flowers faded in the August sunshine.

"This is it," says my father, pointing to the wrought iron bars of an old stone *cantina* attached to a tall building. "This is the house where I was born. I wasn't born at the farm because my mother was on her way to the *cantina* to cook lunch for the priest when she got frightened by a dog. I was the result."

I look at the dusty cement window frame, barred with iron rods and spider webs. With a stick, I gather some of the webs to one side and peer in the open space. It's a low room with cement walls and a mud floor. In one corner is a small stack of kindling, in another corner is a rusted cement mixer. The outside wall has dark streaks on it, where the smoke from the fire smudged the grey cement as it spiralled upward.

"The priest owned this house. He let my mother use it for cooking and sometimes when Papa and Giacomo and Americo worked late in the fields behind the church, they came here to sleep. They weren't supposed to, but you know.... The day I was born, he wasn't too happy. He didn't get his lunch that day."

We continue en route and get as far as the Bar Italia, where Rocco calls out, "*Mezzabotte*, come! I have a surprise for you. Look, it's your old friend, Angelo."

Angelo wears blue jeans, a T-shirt, a baseball cap and a big smile. He's the same height as my father. Angelo and my father begin to catch up, hands flying, memories bursting into the August heat. Then my father starts to laugh so hard he spews his beer across the metal table. Reaching for his hanky, he wipes his mouth then starts roaring all over again. His face is red by the time he's gained control.

"It's the engagement picture," he says to me, shaking his head. "I wish your aunt Regina was here. She was the one who said we had to send that picture."

He was 34 years old when he and my mother got engaged. They had gone to a photographer on Dundas Street, not Italian, but with a nice studio with a fancy velvet chair and Roman pillars. The photographer took the picture and they paid and arranged for the photographer to send the picture to his parents in Supino.

"Now, Angelo tells me the picture caused a scandal in Supino. *Scandalo*. In the photo your mother was sitting beside me, like this." He reaches over and puts his right hand on top of mine. "You see?" he says. In those days, you were not supposed to be touching a woman before you were married. Here he was touching her and sending a photo for everyone to see.

Before we leave the bar we promise to go to Angelo's house for lunch the next day. I am thinking how nice it was of Rocco to set up a meeting with Angelo and my father, when my father says with a chuckle, "I don't know this guy Angelo. Never saw him before in my life."

Early the next morning, Bob and I go for a walk and discover a small sanctuary about the size of a telephone booth. Beneath a grotto shell made of plaster is a statue of the Virgin Mary surrounded by several vases of carnations and four rows of votive candles. The sign stuck in the ground beside the sanctuary says: MADONNA DI LORETO.

Later, at the Bar Italia, Rocco says, "*Madonna di Loreto*? I tell you all the facts. Years ago, a man left Supino and went to Detroit. Every letter he writes he tells about snow and gangsters. Then, suddenly, the man gets sick. We hear nothing more. After many months a poster goes up in front of the municipal building, announcing that the politicians are bringing a statue from Loreto. It's after the war and there is no money for bread, let alone statues. The Supinese cast curses on the heads of the politicians. Curses as steady as rain.

"Eventually we hear the explanation. One evening, as the man from Detroit lay dying in the hospital, the *Madonna di Loreto* came to visit him. It was December. In

Detroit, people were shovelling snow, but in Italy the villagers from Loreto were setting the bonfires to light the way for the Holy Family and the sacred house. The man from Detroit begs for the Madonna's help. The Virgin nods. The man gets better. He's back in his own bed before the new year arrives. He sends money to the *municipio* to bring a statue from Loreto to Supino as a thank-you to the Madonna for saving his life. Now every December we build bonfires on the road from Morolo to Supino and over to the *autostrada* to show the Holy Family the way to their house."

My father's brother, Americo, 13 years older, "stole" his wife Giovanna from Morolo when the woman's affluent parents refused to allow their daughter to marry a poor Coletta. When she was taken, presumably against her will, they had no choice but to marry her as quickly as possible to avoid scandal. Americo was the same brother who asked his new wife to hold out her apron under the cherry tree while he dropped the fruit into the white canopy below. They called out endearments to each other and were teased by their younger siblings, but Americo confided later to my father in private that, "It's better to have a good woman to sleep with than a cow."

My father says now, "Sometimes when I walked home from the market in Frosinone or Morolo and I was too tired to climb the hill to the farmhouse, I'd stay with Americo. His kids were young, but Americo let them stay up late sitting around the fire listening to ghost stories. Sometimes you could hear the werewolves howling in the night. Their voices weren't as sweet as his wife's, who sang beautifully.

Americo liked to buy song sheets for Giovanna at fairs in the neighbouring villages. Then, she'd sing for all of us."

❖

The next day, while we were at the bar for morning coffee, a navy Mercedes stops out front and a man dressed in Armani and carrying a Louis Vuitton briefcase emerges. The workers offer him a chair, a coffee, but he waves their polite gestures aside. Instead, he pulls out papers from his briefcase and instructs the workers. He speaks arrogantly. He is the official representative of the Lazio tourist office coordinating and funding the feast of San Antonio.

He slides his sunglasses down the bridge of his suntanned nose, appraises me and in a husky voice full of innuendo, murmurs, "Allow me to present you with my card, Madam." His manicured fingers catch my hand. "And you are?"

"My wife," replies Bob.

The workers finally smile. Returning to the table, the stranger gives a few instructions. The villagers all nod their heads and say, "*Sí. Sí.*" Then the stranger returns to his car, drives off and the tension dissolves like exhaust fumes. The workers have humoured him, listened to his plans, but the lights and the ribbons will be put up the same way they have always been. The decorations are made of light balsam wood and cut into the shape of tulips, doves and water fountains. The ornaments are as wide as the street. The window workers secure the wooden shapes with pieces of blue nylon rope, tying them to shutters, or metal pipes, or whatever's handy.

An older woman appears at the open window. I can barely see her head above the ledge, but I can hear her voice, "No. I had that one last year. Give me the water fountain. I don't care. Take it down if you have to. You're Graziella's son, no? Listen to me, bigga shot." Then, there's a loud bang, like the old lady has slammed her walking stick onto the floor. "On the head of San Antonio, I swear, if I have to come down there...." There's a quick shuffle and the water fountain is handed up to her window. Tiny lights edge its wooden frame.

We walk past the pizza shop where a line is forming, customers shouting *"Duemila"* to order 2,000 lire worth of pizza. The baker stops to wipe his forehead and when he looks up he sees my father.

"Mezzabotte. Mezzabotte," he calls. "So, it is true. You have returned. Wait. I call my wife." By the time his wife comes out of the hot, steamy kitchen, there is bedlam in the Supino bakery. The butcher from across the street yells over that we're from Toronto. A woman walking past stops to ask if we know her cousin, who lives in Woodbridge. The sun's high in the sky by the time we leave the bakery. I have a pizza in my hand, Bob has a six-pack of *aranciata* drinks, my father has the address of the bakery people in his back pocket. We're going there for lunch tomorrow.

We bump into men hanging posters by the church that announce there's a concert tonight in honour of the feast of San Antonio, but the date stated is a week old. Despite this lack of logic my father assures us, "Everyone knows the date. It's the same every year. The procession, the celebrations, all the same. So the poster, it's not so important except that it's a very fine portrait of San Antonio."

Inside a side door to the church vestibule is a sheer white lace curtain, a small mahogany table with curved and spindly legs, a lamp, a guest book and a fountain pen lying ready.

A priest appears from behind the curtain and welcomes us. "This display exhibits handiwork from the beginning of the century. All of these pieces were donated to the church and preserved in their original form. Please feel free to look around and sign the guest book."

I touch the white crocheted altar cloth, turning under the edge to read the name: Corsi, Filomena Maria, 1926. Did my grandmother make this? It's a narrow cloth, the material a little rough with small loops and imperfections in the weave. Along the edges are scallops, like the petals of a wild rose. A silver thread sparkles in the light, winking in and out of the hem.

"Do you know about this cloth?" I ask my father.

"Well sure. Your grandmother made it. She sewed a piece of her hair in the corner — you know, like signing a painting."

We wander out; I am thinking about my grandmother by the fireside crocheting, Bob has his eye on the *porchetta* cart nearby. Under a glass case lies a roasted pig with a lemon in its mouth. A man stands with a knife in his hand, ready. With the other hand, he stirs a mixture of red peppers and chubby mushrooms on an oily grill.

"There might not be anything to do in Supino," says Linda, "but have you noticed there's always something to eat?"

The ubiquitous Rocco spots us from across the street and asks my father as he is approaching, "*Mezzabotte*, do you know the family Nichilo? They live above the post office. Next month they go to Toronto. First time away from Supino. First airplane ride. They are very anxious about the trip. Worried about lots of little things. That is why I am going to their house today to inspect the suitcase. The woman is worried about the luggage. Is it big enough to hold everything for two weeks? Or maybe it's too big?"

My father says, "I'll stop in and see them later."

The church bell begins to swing. Low, mournful sounds fill the narrow pathways of Supino. People gather in the *piazza* and the bars fall silent. The bells are swinging steadily now and incense floats from the doorway of the church.

Rows of altar boys parade through heavy wooden doors; men in red robes march behind. On their shoulders are two long poles and a platform of split logs where the statue of San Antonio rests. The villagers begin to sing, a tune from centuries ago, soft and sorrowful. Men hold their hats in their hands; women drape rosaries between their fingers. An old woman is tossing dried rose petals from her window. They float in the warm August air, tumbling slowly, leisurely weaving their way to the ground. Petals surround the Saint as he passes. As the altar boys step on them, their perfume mixes with the sharper scent of the incense. My eyes burn with tears.

I suddenly realize my father is no longer standing nearby and scan the crowd for his frail frame. I duck down the nearest laneway and the scent of tomato sauce with olive oil and *basilico* and red wine greets me as I pass planter boxes spilling over with pepper plants. Card tables, plastic patio tables and heavy oak tables with ornately carved legs are adorned with checkered cloths and decanters of red wine. The patio is brimming with men in conversation and at first I can't find my father. Then, from a side doorway, he enters carrying a bowl of spaghetti.

"The priest's family used to live here. They wanted to thank my mother for all her cooking, so one day a year, on the feast of San Antonio — did I tell you the priest's name was Antonio? — they arranged for a feast: spaghetti, veal, chicken, wine. Music and dancing and singing follow the meal. That's what's going on here tonight," my father says, as if he expected it all along.

Outside, the lights of San Antonio shine suspended in the dark Supino sky. An outlined water fountain showers tiny white lights against an ebony backdrop. Suddenly, a burst of colour illuminates the sky. A million shooting stars jump from the mountaintop and rain down on the bell tower of the church.

At the Ferentino market the next day, Bob and I discover a carpenter's shop. An intoxicating aroma of wood shavings and beeswax wafts through the door. Inside the doorway is a beautiful pine buffet and hutch. I slide my hand along the silky surface of the knotty pine boards, caress the round wooden doorknobs, inhale the alluring scent of fresh sawdust. The woman in charge says it is $350, but

Bob doesn't use the next phrase as Joe instructed him to, "*Troppo!* Too much!" which should always be said loudly, in disbelief, preferably with a smack to your forehead to reinforce your point. Instead, Bob says to me, "Ask her if they'll deliver," but I've no idea how to say that.

I point to the buffet, make a lifting motion with my hands and do the universal gesture for driving, two hands on an invisible steering wheel in front of me. The woman seems to understand. She repeats the price and we say, "*Sí, sí,*" and she walks to the door, looks at our car and laughs. I suggest we just write down our address, give her the money and hope for the best. Bob draws a map for the woman and she nods and says, "*No problema.*" We pay two thirds up front and pray the buffet will arrive.

We continue our walk to the market and as we get closer, brightly-coloured awnings hail the bargaining of villagers and merchants. Triangular mountains of peaches tower over valleys of rosy strawberries, chubby purple eggplants snuggle close to rows of slim and shiny zucchini and piles of prickly artichokes. Fresh-cut pineapple scents the air. There are wheels of *parmigiano*, triangles of romano, fish in waxy paper, ceramic crocks of green olives in brine, wrinkled black olives, olives in garlic-studded oil, olives with whole chili peppers and black peppercorns.

The market casts its web for miles up side streets, down laneways, throughout *piazzas* promising bolts of fabric, copper pots, every size of screw and nail, goat's bells, bathing suits, prosciutto slicers, religious candles, leather harnesses, bed sheets, grapevine pruners, baby highchairs with wicker seats, bocce balls, hair dye, and at the edge of the *piazza* in front of a church, hot, freshly-roasted peanuts.

Back at the house, Joe admonishes, "Bob. Maria. Why you sit in the house all alone? Come, it's time for lunch. Your father and Kathryn, they already there. We wait for you."

After I tell Joe, delicately, about the buffet he points out that there is no kitchen, therefore no dishes, therefore no need for the buffet. When I suggest that perhaps a small kitchen sink could be installed he instantly says, "I have one in my garage. I put it in myself this afternoon."

A man joins us at the table, accepts a glass of wine from Angela, a plate of fettuccine and salad, pushes the reluctant lettuce leaves onto his fork with a piece of coarse bread. Finally he gets to the point of his visit. Joe translates.

"Sergio here says there's a truck at the Kennedy Bar. The driver's looking for a *Canadese* with curly hair and glasses. He's got a cupboard for him."

Outside a horn beeps, a moment later the doorbell rings and as Angela pushes open the kitchen window we hear the voices of the neighbours in the street below. Our buffet has arrived. This time, the question is not where to put the buffet, the question is why the *Canadese* would buy a cupboard to keep dishes when they have no sink to wash dishes. And that leads, of course, back to the original paradox of a house without a kitchen. Down on the street, where so many of our personal decisions are made by the villagers, no one rushes forward eagerly to help unload the buffet. The villagers just stand there, maybe one or two of them shake their heads. A house without a kitchen. And now, a kitchen cupboard for a house without a kitchen. Unbelievable.

"Peppe. Massimo," calls Joe, motioning them to his garage. When they emerge with a stainless steel sink in their arms, a wave of relief blows across the narrow street. Now, the neighbours admire the buffet, running their hands over the polished wood, tapping their knuckles on the glass cupboard doors, checking the wooden knobs on the drawers. Mario's wife holds up one finger. "*Aspetta!*" she warns, lifting the corner of her apron to wipe a smudge off the glass door before we are allowed to unload our purchase.

The neighbours see Bob pay the driver the remaining $150, but believe it to be the total price, so instead of saying, "*Troppo!*" they congratulate Bob, shaking his hand and saying, "*Bravo, Bob. Bravo.*" Even Joe, who knows the real price of the buffet, stands back with his arms crossed over his chest, full of pride. After all, Joe taught Bob everything he needs to know about buying furniture. "*Grazie. Beve?*" Bob suggests, lifting an invisible glass to his lips and the next thing I know we're all down at the Bar Italia toasting our new cupboard and — for the first time — Bob is allowed to pay for the drinks.

On our last day in Supino my father decides he wants to buy a gift for his nephew, Guido — six plastic lawn chairs.

"My cousin has a garden centre," says Rocco. "Right beside the *pensione*. You can't miss it." Obviously I can miss it. Beside the *pensione* is a big stucco house with a long driveway that leads to a triple car garage. In the surrounding field, a herd of cows graze beneath the branches of a chestnut tree. My father pushes the button on the wrought-iron fence post. The gate and the garage doors open. We wander up rows of patio tables, down aisles of lawn chairs. I choose six plastic chairs for Guido and head to the cash register.

"I'll take these chairs, please."

"*Certo*. Rocco told me you were coming. I have your bench right here."

"But I want these lawn chairs."

"The bench is better. Luca. Gianni." Two little boys jump up from beneath a patio table. They carry a white bench along the aisle toward the door, round the corner with a flash of blue jeans and a length of yellow rope. Then the bench and the boys are gone. A woman comes out of the house with a tray of glasses. Rocco's cousin uncorks a bottle. After an hour in the sunshine and several glasses of *Asti Spumante* and strawberries, our faces match their rosy colour. There's a large cardboard box tied to the roof of our car. On the side of the box it says, "Easy assembly." Rocco's cousin hands my father a screwdriver.

Sunbeams filter through the lacy leaves of the quince tree in Guido's yard. The air is still. On the ground rests a grape leaf. As my father assembles the bench he hums the score from "*La Bohéme*." Guido whistles along. When the screws are tightened, they flip the bench with a flourish and sit together, their arms on each other's shoulders. Their white hair, clear blue-grey eyes, Roman nose, gentle smile, that nonchalant shrug of the shoulders when Bob suggests a photo — cut from the same cloth. I have that photograph on the wooden mantle now.

"Maria," says Guido, "for *molti anni*, many years, my house has been the only place in the village with a sign that says Coletta. Then you come. You buy the little house and you put a sign: BOB MCLEAN, MARIA COLETTA MCLEAN. I am very happy to see another Coletta sign in this village. Now you bring *zio* Loreto, my only uncle, back to Italy and you bring Bob and Linda and Kathryn. Suddenly, we are *una famiglia grande*, a big family. Many Colettas in the village; that's the way it should be."

My father walks slowly down the hill of Via Condotto Vecchio toward the village. The sun is approaching the top of Santa Serena so its shadow stretches long and cool down our street. I can hear the clinking of the coins in his pocket slowly fade as he turns toward the *tabacchi* store. Bob and I go into the garden and plan the placement of forget-me-nots, tulips, daffodils, blue and purple morning glories. We decide to check the street for signs of my father and run into *signora* Francesca as she hurries over with her apron held carefully out in front of her. "*Le uova*," she says, stretching the hem of her cotton apron toward us. Nestled in the cloth are half a dozen brown eggs, fresh from her chicken coop, bits of straw still stuck to them.

"*Grazie*," I say, transferring the eggs into my hands.

"That's okay," calls Angela from her kitchen window. "I cook them up for you. Make a sand-a-wich. You eat it tomorrow on the plane. That airplane food. Not so good."

My father has returned, a can of brass polish in his hand. "You polish the door knob for good luck. Plus," he continues, as he flicks a white cloth with a flourish, "if I polish the door knob, I know I come back. *Ritorniamo insieme*."

He continues to work, then says, "When the cherries are almost ripe, there's a feast in this village. *Festa di San Cataldo*. That's a saint who came from Ireland. People walk to Supino the day before the feast and sleep in the fields behind San Sebastiano. Some people bring things to sell. Like a fair. In the morning, for the mass, the church is full of people. Some people have to stand outside in the dark at three or four o'clock in the morning. I used to go first to church, then I would come home to get Giardinella and we'd go to the mountain just as the sun was coming up. On the feast day, there was no work. Every year, early in the morning, the committee came for my father. They wanted him to carry the statue. It was an honour. They gave him a red robe. Later, they build a big fire in front of San Nicola. Roast a pig, or something. There are also biscuits like your aunt Regina used to make, *ginettes*. Some candy brought from Abruzzo, with nuts. Lemons from Sorrento. Fireworks."

"Is that when they cook polenta?" I ask, remembering a fragment of a story he told me about the villagers cooking a huge pot of yellow cornmeal.

"No, no," he says, patiently. "That's the polenta and sausage festival. That's a festival for cold weather — not until January. I don't even like polenta. *Pazzo* Lorenzo, you know, crazy Larry, he got the idea one year that he would stir the polenta. That was a bad idea, but nobody wants to say no to him. He had a big paddle he had made from an old two-by-four. Some people said it was an oar, you know, from a boat. They said he stole it. But that's crazy. Who's got a boat in Supino? The wood was pretty rough and maybe it had been sitting outside all winter because the bottom was caked with mud. *Pazzo* Lorenzo wouldn't let anyone touch it, to wipe the dirt off. When the water started to boil, they poured in the corn meal and crazy Larry stirred. All by himself. Wouldn't let anyone else put a stick in the pot. By the time the polenta's cooked, the paddle's all broken. Everybody's got polenta with sticks in it. Like eating toothpicks.

"The *mostra delle azalee* is the beautiful *festa*. Everyone brings their azalea to the *piazza* outside the church. Some pots are so big, you need two, maybe three people to carry them. You have to come early or there's no room. There's a mass in the morning and in the evening everyone walks among the plants, admiring them and choosing their favourites before the flowers are judged. Finally the cannons in the mountains, left over from the war, are shot off."

Benito walks across the street, pushing a wheelbarrow full of potted plants, 12 plants too many for this yard. My father takes the plants from Benito's arms one at a time and sets them on the patio, then points to the strip of soil between our terrazzo patio and the neighbour's wall. It's a small space about a foot wide and 10 feet long before it plunges down the ravine. This is where I had intended to put my spring bulbs and morning glory vines. Benito gestures to the plants, bowing slightly, as if he's introducing them to me. I don't see a single flower, just tomato plants, pepper plants, rosemary and another that looks suspiciously like a grapevine. Benito sets some plants, very carefully, on the back steps, the others he lines along the perimeter of the yard. Then he stands, a shy smile on his face, waiting for my reaction to his gift. I say, *"Bellissimo,"* and nod my agreement.

Joe comes walking through *signor* Mario's woodlot, carrying a banana tree. Over Benito's shoulder I see Angela coming into the house with a tray of pastries, two bottles of wine and tucked under her elbow, a sleeve of plastic glasses. Behind her are Guido and Luigina. A small group of villagers are climbing up the hill toward the mountain: Christina from the *tabacchi* store, the mailman, some neighbourhood children. At the same time, *signor* Mario, wearing his white shirt, his hair freshly combed, and *signora* Francesca, in her navy spotted dress, without an apron, step out of their house and head down the hill.

The village is coming to say goodbye. They crowd the living room, sit in rows on the marble steps. Children run up and down the front stairs, playing hopscotch. There are three or four people on the verandah. Angela has put glasses and plates of cookies on the kitchen table, but every villager has brought something with them. You can hardly see the wooden mantle for bottles of homemade wine and cognac. Christina, from the *tabacchi* store, hands out lollipops to the children. *Signora* Francesca circulates a basket full of cookies, sweet with anisette-flavoured icing. In the corner, behind the front door, is a burlap sack of hazelnuts. Someone brings a sack of prickly chestnut skins, mulch for the garden to keep the moisture in the ground.

Benito and my father go to Joe's garage, returning in a few minutes with a string of lights. After my father plugs them in behind the fridge, he hooks the lights over the open back door and hands the remaining coil of lights to Benito to string over a tree before he flicks the switch. They're Chinese lanterns, papery houses of blue and red and yellow, swaying brightly in the black Supinese sky. At midnight the church bells ring. The crowds fall silent and we stand together listening to the mournful sound as it leaves the huge brass bell of the church of Santa Maria Maggiore and rolls up the hill, past our house, on its way to the mountain. By the time the 12th bell has rung, the villagers are in the street, waving farewell. "Safe journey. *Buon viaggio*. Come again, *Mezzabotte*." And then, they are gone.

Modificazioni e vidimazioni
delle Autorità italiane.

Arrivederci Mezzabotte

On the first of December, a Tuesday night, the phone rings and Bob answers it, says, "It's your mother." I check my watch. Nine o'clock — too late for her to be calling. Something's wrong.

"Your father says he's sick. Come and do something about him."

I'm struggling with my jacket as I open the front door and step into the cold night. In the yellow light shining from my living room windows, I stare at the rectangular cement stones that lead to their house next door. When I get inside, my father's lying on his back on the floor outside the bathroom door. He's wearing white long johns and his body is so pale and so flat that at first I don't realize he is actually there; I think my mother has spread the damp clothes on the linoleum to dry.

"What's wrong, Dad?" I ask, kneeling beside him and feeling for his pulse. His skin is cool.

"I don't feel so good."

I look up toward the black telephone in the hallway,

but Bob's already there, dialling the numbers, giving the address. He's barely hung up the receiver, when I hear the distant sound of the siren. In minutes the ambulance attendant is kneeling beside me, nudging me out of the way. She says she can't find a vein to stick the IV into. My mother speaks from the living room to complain about the mess they're making in the house, moving the kitchen table to get the stretcher in and cluttering the floor with the wrappers from the needles and the oxygen mask. When I look up at her, she's wringing her hands in her lap.

They won't let me come in the ambulance; they say I can follow in my own car. I speak to my father as they lift him into the ambulance, "It's okay, Dad. You're going to ride in the ambulance. Bob and I will come in our car."

"Well, sure. I'm feeling better."

That's the last thing he says to me. Just before they close the ambulance door, start up the wailing siren, I tell the female attendant to tell my father, "Your daughter says, '*Ti amo.*'" I tell her that he knows what it means.

At the hospital, in the emergency room, my father slips into an endless sleep. He dies as gently as he lived. His death disturbs no one.

Three days later, driving home from the funeral parlour, we pass through Toronto streets lined with coloured holiday lights. In my father's hometown, there is a feast before Christmas. The heavy bells of San Nicola echo through the dark narrow pathways of Supino. The men, dressed in their festive red robes, carry the Saint of Special Favours on a wooden platform, long poles resting on their shoulders. The villagers place gifts of bread, or *ciambella*, at the Saint's feet and offer silent prayers. The procession passes slowly. Every house has a light that illuminates the path where the Saint will pass. Many years ago, my grandparents placed candles at the end of the grape-lined laneway that led to their farm, now the villagers turn on electric lights. Everyone is hushed, solemn, wrapped in emotion. When the procession passes, you may feel a shiver, a sign from the Saint that your favour has been granted.

Acknowledgments

Thank you to my father, for telling me his stories; to Bruce Powe, my creative writing professor at York University, who provided encouragement and friendship; to Michelle Hammer, Bryna Wasserman and Collette Yvonne, friends in my writing circle who asked questions, requested rewrites, believed in me; to my brother, Don Coletta, for reading the first draft and encouraging me to send it to a publisher; to my sister, Linda Willcocks, who shared those 10 days in Supino with us and suggested the title for the book; to my cousins, Johnny and Suzy Paglia, who provided Italian translations, family stories and photographs; to my husband, Bob, and my daughter, Kathryn, who humoured me through the lonely writing days and the fits of doubt, the joys and disappointments; to my agent, Carolyn Swayze, who believed in me, inspired me and became my friend; to Carol Watterson and Joy Gugeler and the staff at Raincoast Books for making my first publishing experience a wonderful adventure.